THIS BOOK BELONGS TO

Marybeth Buskirk

LEARN FROM THE
GREAT TEACHER

LEARN FROM THE
GREAT TEACHER

"Let the young children come to me,
and do not try to stop them."
—Luke 18:16.

·WHAT CHILDREN NEED FROM PARENTS·

ALL parents participate in an event that is beyond full human understanding. They each contribute a part of themselves. As a result, what develops within the mother is a fully formed living person. It is not surprising, therefore, that when a baby is born, people speak of the event as "the miracle of birth."

Of course, producing children is only the beginning of the responsibility of parents. At first, human babies are almost entirely dependent, but as they grow, they need more than physical attention. They need help to develop mentally, emotionally, morally, and spiritually.

To realize wholesome development, children especially need the love of parents. Although verbal expressions of love are important, actions need to back up the words. Yes, children need a good parental example. They need moral guidance, principles by which to live. And they need these from their tender years on. Heartbreaking things can and do happen when children do not receive help until it is too late.

The best principles that can be found anywhere are those found in the Bible. Instruction based on the Bible has unique advantages. Through such instruction, children come to realize that what they are being told is, not what some human says, but what their Creator, their heavenly Father, says. This gives the counsel strength that cannot be equaled.

The Bible encourages parents to work hard to impress right principles on the minds of their children. As children grow older, however, parents often find it difficult to talk with them about things that matter the most. This book, *Learn From the Great Teacher,* is designed to help prevent such a situation from developing. It will provide you and your children with spiritual material to read together. But more than that, it should stimulate conversation between young ones and those who read this book with them.

You will notice that the book calls for a response on the part of children. Many well-placed questions are provided in the printed material. When you come to these, you will see a dash (—). This is a reminder to pause and encourage the child to express himself. Children like to be involved. Without that involvement, a child will quickly lose interest.

More important, though, these questions will help you to learn what is on the child's mind. True, the child may come out with answers that are not correct. But the printed material that follows each question is designed to help the child to develop wholesome patterns of thinking.

A special feature of the book is its more than 230 pictures. Most of these have captions that call for a response from the child, based on what he sees and has read. So review the pictures with the child. They can be a fine teaching aid that will drive home the lessons being taught.

When the child learns to read, encourage him to read the book to you as well as to himself. The more he reads it, the more its good counsel will be impressed on his mind and heart. But to strengthen the bonds of affection and respect between you and your child, by all means read the book together, and do it regularly.

In a way that seemed almost unimaginable a few decades ago, children are exposed to illicit sex, spiritism, and other degrading practices. So they need protection, which this book helps to provide in a dignified yet straightforward manner. Yet, children especially need to be directed to the Source of all wisdom, our heavenly Father, Jehovah God. This is what Jesus, the Great Teacher, always did. We sincerely hope that this book will help you and your family to mold your lives so as to be pleasing to Jehovah, to your eternal blessing.

· CONTENTS ·

Chapter		Page

CHAPTER 1

WHY JESUS WAS A GREAT TEACHER

MORE than two thousand years ago, a very special child was born who grew up to become the greatest man who ever lived. No one living way back then had airplanes or automobiles. There were no such things as televisions, computers, and the Internet.

The child was given the name Jesus. He became the wisest man ever to walk the earth. Jesus also became the best teacher. He would explain difficult things in ways that made them easy to understand.

Jesus taught people everywhere he met them. He taught them at the seashore and on boats. He taught them in homes and when traveling. Jesus did not have a car, nor did he travel by bus or train. Jesus walked from place to place, teaching people.

We learn many things from other people. But we can learn the most important things from the Great Teacher, Jesus. It is in the Bible that Jesus' words are found. When we hear those words from the Bible, it is just as if Jesus were talking to us.

Why was Jesus such a Great Teacher? One reason is that Jesus himself had been taught. And he knew how important it is to listen. But to whom did Jesus listen? Who taught him?— His Father did. And Jesus' Father is God.

Before coming to earth as a man, Jesus lived in heaven with God. So Jesus was different from other men because no other man lived in heaven before being born on earth. In heaven Jesus had been a good Son, one who listened to his Father. Jesus was therefore able to teach people what he had learned from God. By listening to your father and mother, you can copy Jesus.

Another reason why Jesus was a Great Teacher is that he loved people. He wanted to help people learn about God. Jesus loved grown-ups, but he loved children too. And children liked to be with Jesus because he would talk to them and listen to them.

Why did children like to be with Jesus?

One day some parents brought their young children to Jesus. But his friends thought that the Great Teacher was too busy to speak with little children. So they told them to go away. But what did Jesus say?— Jesus said: "Let the young children come to me; do not try to stop them." Yes, Jesus wanted the young children to come to him. So even though he was a very wise and important man, Jesus took time to teach little children.—Mark 10:13, 14.

Do you know why Jesus taught children and listened to them? One reason is that he wanted to make them happy by telling them things about God, his heavenly Father. How can you make people happy?— By telling them things that you have learned about God.

One time, Jesus used a little child to teach His friends an important lesson. He took the child and stood him in the middle of His disciples, who were His followers. Then Jesus said that these grown men must change their ways and become like this little one.

What did Jesus mean when he said that? Do you know how a grown man, or even a little older child, should become like a small child?— Well, a small child does not know as much as an older person and is willing to learn. So Jesus was saying that his disciples need to be humble, as small children are. Yes, we can all learn many things from other people. And we should all realize that the teachings of Jesus are more important than our own ideas.—Matthew 18:1-5.

Another reason why Jesus was such a Great Teacher is that he knew how to make things interesting to people. He explained things in a simple, clear way. He spoke about birds and flowers and other ordinary things to help people understand about God.

What lesson can older children and grown-ups learn from a small child?

12

*What lesson was Jesus teaching
when he spoke of birds and flowers?*

One day when Jesus was on a mountainside, many people came to him. Jesus sat down and gave a talk, or sermon, to them, as you can see here. This talk is called the Sermon on the Mount. He said: 'Look at the birds in the sky. They do not plant seed. They do not store food in houses. But God in heaven feeds them. Are you not worth more than they are?'

Jesus also said: 'Take a lesson from the lilies of the field. They grow without working. And see how beautiful they are! Even rich King Solomon was not dressed more beautifully than the lilies of the field. So if God takes care of the flowers that grow, will he not also take care of you?'—Matthew 6:25-33.

Do you understand the lesson Jesus was teaching?— He did not want us to worry about where we would get food to eat or clothes to put on. God knows that we need all those things.

Jesus did not say that we should not work for food and clothing. But he said that we should put God first. If we do that, God will see to it that we have food to eat and clothing to wear. Do you believe that?—

When Jesus finished talking, what did the people think?— The Bible says that they were amazed at his way of teaching. It was very interesting to listen to him. What he said helped people to do what is right.—Matthew 7:28.

"This is my Son . . .
Listen to him"

So it is very important that we learn from Jesus. Do you know how we can do that?— Well, we have his sayings written in a book. Do you know what that book is?— It is the Holy Bible. This means we can listen to Jesus by paying attention to the things that we read in the Bible. In fact, the Bible has an exciting story about how God himself told us to listen to Jesus. Let's see what happened.

One day Jesus took three of his friends high up into a mountain. Their names were James, John, and Peter. We will learn a lot more about these men later on, since all three of them were close friends of Jesus. But on this special occasion, Jesus' face began to shine brightly. And his clothes became as brilliant as light, as you can see here.

Afterward, a voice from heaven was heard by Jesus and his friends. It said: "This is my Son, the beloved, whom I have approved; listen to him." (Matthew 17:1-5) Do you know whose voice that was?— It was God's voice! Yes, it was God who said that they should listen to his Son.

What about us today? Will we obey God and listen to his Son, the Great Teacher?— That is what we all need to do. Do you remember how we can do that?—

Yes, we can listen to God's Son by reading the Bible accounts of his life. There are many wonderful things that the Great Teacher has to tell us. You will enjoy learning these things that are written in the Bible. And it will also bring you happiness if you tell your friends the good things you learn.

For more fine thoughts about the good things that come from listening to Jesus, open your Bible and read John 3:16; 8:28-30; and Acts 4:12.

CHAPTER 2

A LETTER FROM A LOVING GOD

TELL me, which book do you like best of all?— Some children would pick one that tells about animals. Others would choose a book with lots of pictures in it. It can be fun to read those books.

But the best books in all the world are the ones that tell us the truth about God. One of those books is more precious than all the others. Do you know which one it is?— The Bible.

Why is the Bible so important?— Because it came from God. It tells us about him and about the good things that he will do for us. And it shows us what we should do in order to please him. It is like a letter from God.

Now God could have written the whole Bible in heaven and then given it to man. But he didn't. Even though the ideas came from God, he used his servants on earth to do most of the writing of the Bible.

How did God do that?— To understand how, consider this. When we hear the voice of someone on the radio, the voice may come from a person who is far away. When we watch television, we can even see pictures of people in other countries of the world, and we can hear what they are saying.

Men can even go all the way to the moon in their spaceships, and they can send messages back to the earth from there. Did you know that?— If men can do that, can God send messages from heaven?— Of course he can! And he did it long before men had radio or television.

Moses was a man who actually heard God speak. Moses could not see God, but he could hear God's voice. Millions of people were there when this happened. In fact, on that day God caused a whole mountain to shake, and there was thunder and lightning. The people knew that God had spoken, but they were very scared. So they told Moses: "Let not God speak with us for fear we may die." Later, Moses wrote down the things that God had said. And what Moses wrote is in the Bible.—Exodus 20:18-21.

Moses wrote the first five books of the Bible. But he was not the only one who wrote. God used about 40 men to write parts

How do we know that God can speak to us from far away?

of the Bible. These men lived a long, long time ago, and it took many years for the Bible to be finished. Yes, it took a period of about 1,600 years! What is amazing is that even though some of these men never met one another, everything they wrote is in absolute agreement.

Some men who were used by God to write the Bible were famous. Although Moses had been a shepherd, he became the leader of the nation of Israel. Solomon was a king who was both the wisest and the richest man in the world. But other writers were not so well-known. Amos took care of trees that grew figs.

In addition, one Bible writer was a medical doctor. Do you know his name?— It was Luke. Another writer had been a tax collector. His name was Matthew. Still another had been a lawyer, an expert in Jewish religious law. He wrote more books of the Bible than anyone else. Do you know his name?— It was Paul. And Jesus' disciples Peter and John, who also were Bible writers, had been fishermen.

Many of these Bible writers wrote about things that God was going to do in the future. How did they know those things before they even happened?— God had given those men the information. He had told them what would happen.

By the time that Jesus, the Great Teacher, was on earth, a big part of the Bible had been written. Now, remember, the Great Teacher had been in heaven. He knew what God had done. Did he believe that the Bible was from God?— Yes, he did.

When Jesus talked to people about the works of God, he read from the Bible. Sometimes he told them from memory what it said. Jesus also brought us more information from God.

Jesus said: "The very things I heard from him I am speaking in the world." (John 8:26) Jesus had heard many things from God because he had lived with God. And where can we read those things that Jesus said?— In the Bible. It was all written down for us to read.

Of course, when God used men to write, they wrote in the language that they used every day. So most of the Bible was written in Hebrew, some in Aramaic, and a lot of it in Greek. Since most people today do not know how to read those languages, the Bible has been put into other languages. Today parts of the Bible can be read in over 2,260 languages. Just think of that! The Bible is God's letter to people everywhere. But no matter how many times it has been copied, the message is from God.

What are the names of these Bible writers?

What the Bible says is important for us. It was written a long time ago. But it tells about things that are happening today. And it tells us what God is going to do in the near future. What it says is exciting! It gives us a wonderful hope.

The Bible also tells us how God wants us to live. It tells us what is right and what is wrong. You need to know this, and so do I. It tells us about people who did bad things and what happened to them, so that we can avoid the trouble they had. It also tells us about people who did right and the good results that came to them. It was all written down for our good.

What things can you learn from reading the Bible?

But to get the most out of the Bible, we need to know the answer to a question. The question is this: Who gave us the Bible? What would you say?— Yes, the whole Bible is from God. How, then, can we show that we are really wise?— By listening to God and by doing what he says.

So we need to take time to read the Bible together. When we get a letter from someone we love very much, we read it again and again. It is precious to us. That is the way the Bible should be to us because it is a letter from the One who loves us most. It is a letter from a loving God.

Take a few more minutes now to read these scriptures that show that the Bible truly is God's Word, written for our benefit: Romans 15:4; 2 Timothy 3:16, 17; and 2 Peter 1:20, 21.

CHAPTER 3

THE ONE WHO MADE ALL THINGS

I KNOW something wonderful. Would you like to hear it?— Look at your hand. Bend your fingers. Now pick something up. Your hand can do many things, and it can do them well. Do you know who made our hands?—

Who made all living things?

Yes, it was the same One who made our mouth, our nose, and our eyes. It was God, the Father of the Great Teacher. Aren't we glad that God gave us eyes?— We can see many things with them. We can look at flowers. We can look at the green grass and the blue sky. We may even see hungry little birds like the ones in the picture. Really, it is marvelous that we can see things like this, isn't it?—

But who made these things? Did some man make them? No. Men can make a house. But no man can make grass that grows. Men cannot make a baby bird, a flower, or any other living thing. Did you know that?—

God is the one who made all these things. God made the heavens and the earth. He made people too. He created the first man and the first woman. Jesus, the Great Teacher, taught this.—Matthew 19:4-6.

Since someone made the house, who made the flowers, the trees, and the animals?

How did Jesus know that God made man and woman? Did Jesus see God do it?— Yes, he did. Jesus was with God when God made man and woman. Jesus was the first person that God made. Jesus was an angel, and he lived in heaven with his Father.

The Bible tells us that God said: "Let us make man." (Genesis 1:26) Do you know whom God was talking to?— He was talking to his Son. He was talking to the one who later came to earth and became Jesus.

Isn't that exciting? Just think! When we listen to Jesus, we are being taught by the one who was with God when God made the earth and all other things. Jesus learned much from working with his Father in heaven. No wonder Jesus is the Great Teacher!

Do you think that God was unhappy about being alone before he made his Son?— No, he wasn't. Well, if he was not unhappy, why did he make other living things?— He did this because he is a God of love. He wanted others to live and enjoy life. We should thank God that he gave us life.

Everything that God has done shows his love. God made the sun. The sun gives us light and keeps us warm. Everything would be cold and there would be no life on earth if we did not have the sun. Aren't you glad that God made the sun?—

God makes it rain too. Sometimes you may not like the rain because you can't go outside to play when it rains. But the rain helps the flowers to grow. So when we see beautiful flowers, whom are we going to thank for them?— God. And to whom should we give thanks when we eat fruits and vegetables that taste good?— We should thank God because it is his sun and rain that make things grow.

Suppose that someone asks you, 'Did God make man and the animals too?' What would you say?— It is correct to say: "Yes, God made man and the animals." But what if someone does not believe that God really made humans? What if he or she says that man came from animals? Well, the Bible does not teach that. It says that God created all living things.—Genesis 1:26-31.

But someone may tell you that he does not believe in God. What will you say then?— Why not point to a house? Ask the person: "Who made that house?" Everyone knows that someone had to make it. The house certainly did not make itself!—Hebrews 3:4.

Then take the person to a garden and show him a flower. Ask him: "Who made this?" No man did. And just as the house did not make itself, so this flower did not make itself either. Someone made it. God did.

Ask the person to stop and listen to the song of a bird. Then ask him: "Who made the birds and taught them to sing?" God did. God is the one who made the heavens and the earth and all living things! He is the One who gives life.

Yet, someone may say that he believes only what he can see. He may say: 'If I can't see it, I don't believe it.' So some people say they don't believe in God because they can't see him.

It is true that we cannot see God. The Bible says: 'No man can see God.' No man, woman, or child on earth can see God. So no one should try to make a picture or an image of God. God even tells us not to make an image of him. So, then, it would not please God for us to have things like that in our house.—Exodus 20:4, 5; 33:20; John 1:18.

But if you cannot see God, how do you know that there really is a God? Think about this. Can you see the wind?— No. Nobody can see the wind. But you can see the things the wind does. You can see the leaves move when the wind blows through the branches of a tree. So you believe that there is wind.

You can see the things God has done too. When you see a living flower or a bird, you see something that God has made. So you believe that there really is a God.

Someone might ask you, 'Who made the sun and the earth?' The Bible says: "God created the heavens and the earth."

(Genesis 1:1) Yes, God made all these wonderful things! How do you feel about that?—

Isn't it wonderful to be alive? We can hear the beautiful songs of the birds. We can see the flowers and the other things that God has made. And we can eat the foods that God has given us.

For all these things, we should thank God. Most of all, we should thank him for giving us life. If we are really thankful to God, we will do something. What is that?— We will listen to God, and we will do what he tells us in the Bible. In that way we can show that we love the One who made all things.

We should show appreciation to God for all that he has done. How? Read what is written at Psalm 139:14 (138:14, "Douay Version"); John 4:23, 24; 1 John 5:21; and Revelation 4:11.

How do you know that there is wind?

CHAPTER 4

GOD HAS A NAME

WHAT is often the first thing you ask someone when you first meet him?— Yes, you ask what his name is. We all have names. God gave the first man on earth a name. He named him Adam. Adam's wife was named Eve.

However, it is not only people who have names. Think about other things that also do. When someone gives you a doll or a pet, you give it a name, don't you?— Yes, having a name is very important.

Look up at the many, many stars at night. Do you think they have names?— Yes, God gave a name to each star in the sky. The Bible tells us: "He is counting the number of the stars; all of them he calls by their names."—Psalm 147:4.

Who would you say is the most important person in the whole universe?— Yes, it is God. Do you think that he has a name?— Jesus said that He does. Jesus once said in prayer to God: 'I have made your name known to my followers.' (John 17: 26) Do you know God's name?— God himself tells us what it is. He says: "I am Jehovah. That is my name." So God's name is JEHOVAH.—Isaiah 42:8.

How does it make you feel when others remember your name?— You are happy, aren't you?— Jehovah wants people to know his name too. So we should use the name Jehovah when we talk about God. The Great Teacher used God's name, Jehovah, when he spoke to people. One time Jesus said: "You must love Jehovah your God with your whole heart."—Mark 12:30.

Jesus knew that "Jehovah" is a very important name. So he taught his followers to use God's name. He even taught them to speak about God's name in their prayers. Jesus knew that God wants all people to know His name, Jehovah.

Long ago God showed the importance of his name to the man Moses, who was one of the sons of Israel. The sons of Israel, who were called Israelites, lived in the land called Egypt. The people of that land were known as Egyptians. They made the Israelites slaves and were very mean to them. When Moses grew up, he tried to help one of his people. This made Pharaoh, the king of Egypt, angry. He wanted to kill Moses! So Moses ran away from Egypt.

Moses went to another land. It was the land of Midian. There Moses got married and began to raise a family.

Did you know that all the stars have names?

He also worked as a shepherd, taking care of sheep. One day Moses was busy caring for his sheep near a mountain when he saw an amazing thing. A thornbush was on fire, but it was not burning up! Moses went closer to get a better look.

Do you know what happened?— Moses heard a voice calling from the middle of that burning thornbush. The voice called out, "Moses! Moses!" Who was saying that?— It was God speaking! God had a lot of work for Moses to do. God said: 'Come and let me send you to Pharaoh, the king of Egypt, and you bring my people, the sons of Israel, out of Egypt.' God promised to help Moses do this.

But Moses said to God: 'Suppose I come to the sons of Israel in Egypt and say that God sent me. What if they ask me, "What is his name?" What shall I say?' God told Moses to tell the sons of Israel: 'Jehovah has sent me to you. Jehovah is my name forever.' (Exodus 3:1-15) This shows that God was going to keep

What important thing did Moses learn
at the burning thornbush?

28

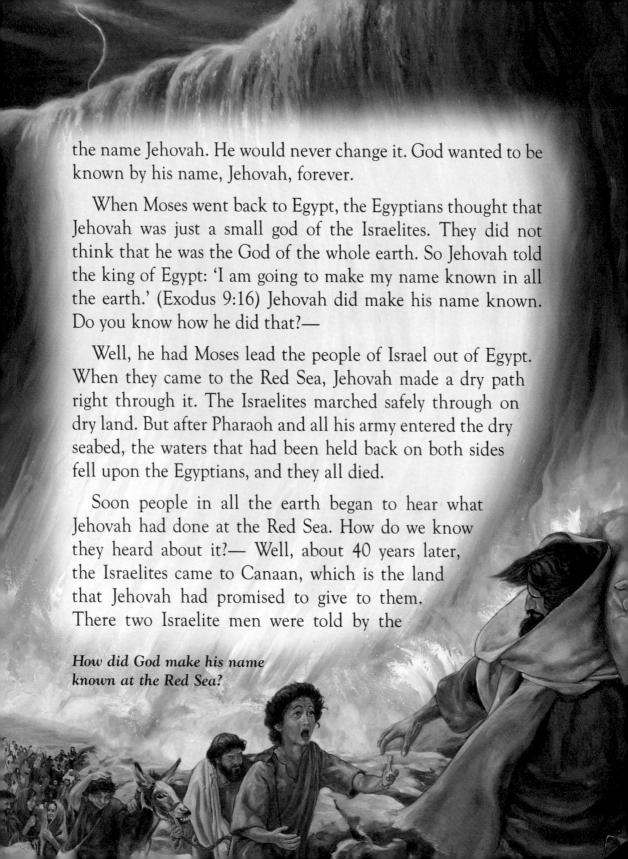

the name Jehovah. He would never change it. God wanted to be known by his name, Jehovah, forever.

When Moses went back to Egypt, the Egyptians thought that Jehovah was just a small god of the Israelites. They did not think that he was the God of the whole earth. So Jehovah told the king of Egypt: 'I am going to make my name known in all the earth.' (Exodus 9:16) Jehovah did make his name known. Do you know how he did that?—

Well, he had Moses lead the people of Israel out of Egypt. When they came to the Red Sea, Jehovah made a dry path right through it. The Israelites marched safely through on dry land. But after Pharaoh and all his army entered the dry seabed, the waters that had been held back on both sides fell upon the Egyptians, and they all died.

Soon people in all the earth began to hear what Jehovah had done at the Red Sea. How do we know they heard about it?— Well, about 40 years later, the Israelites came to Canaan, which is the land that Jehovah had promised to give to them. There two Israelite men were told by the

How did God make his name known at the Red Sea?

young woman Rahab: "We have heard how Jehovah dried up the waters of the Red Sea from before you when you came out of Egypt."—Joshua 2:10.

Today many people are just like those Egyptians. They do not believe that Jehovah is the God of the whole earth. So Jehovah wants his own people to tell others about him. This is what Jesus did. Toward the end of his life on earth, he told Jehovah in prayer: "I have made your name known to them."—John 17:26.

Jesus made God's name known.
Can you point out God's name in the Bible?

Do you want to be like Jesus? Then tell others that God's name is Jehovah. You may find that many people do not know that. So perhaps you can show them the scripture in the Bible at Psalm 83:18. Let's get the Bible right now and find that scripture together. It says: "That people may know that you, whose name is Jehovah, you alone are the Most High over all the earth."

What do we learn from reading this?— Yes, we learn that Jehovah is the most important name there is. It is the name of Almighty God, the Father of Jesus and the One who made all things. And remember, Jesus said that we should love Jehovah God with our whole heart. Do you love Jehovah?—

How can we show that we love Jehovah?— One way is by getting to know him as a Friend. Another way is by telling others what his name is. We can show them right from the Bible that his name is Jehovah. We can also tell about the wonderful things Jehovah has made and the good things he has done. This makes Jehovah very happy because he wants people to know about him. We can have a share in doing that, can't we?—

Not everyone will want to listen when we speak about Jehovah. Many people did not listen even when Jesus, the Great Teacher, talked about Him. But that did not stop Jesus from speaking about Jehovah.

So let's be like Jesus. Let's keep talking about Jehovah. If we do, Jehovah God will be pleased with us because we show love for his name.

Now read together from the Bible a few more texts showing the importance of God's name: Isaiah 12:4, 5; Matthew 6:9; John 17:6; and Romans 10:13.

CHAPTER 5

"THIS IS MY SON"

WHEN children do good things, those who take care of them are pleased. When a girl does something well, her father is glad to be able to tell others: "This is my daughter." Or if a boy does good things, a father is happy to say: "This is my son."

Jesus always does what pleases his Father. So his Father is proud of him. Do you remember what Jesus' Father did one day when Jesus was with three of his followers?— Yes, God spoke all the way from heaven to tell them: "This is my Son, the beloved, whom I have approved."—Matthew 17:5.

Jesus is always happy to do things that please his Father. Do you know why? Because he really loves his Father. If a person does things only because he has to do them, this seems hard. But when he is willing, it is easier. Do you know what it means to be willing?— It means really wanting to do something.

Even before Jesus came to earth, he was willing to do whatever his Father asked him to do. This is because he loves his Father, Jehovah God. Jesus had a wonderful place in heaven with his Father. But God had a special work for Jesus to do. To do that work, Jesus had to leave heaven. He had to be born as a baby on earth. Jesus was willing to do this because Jehovah wanted him to do it.

To be born as a baby on earth, Jesus had to have a mother. Do you know who she was?— Her name was Mary. Jehovah sent his angel Gabriel from heaven to talk to Mary. Gabriel told

*What did the angel Gabriel
tell Mary?*

her that she was going to have a
baby boy. The baby would be
named Jesus. And who would
the baby's father be?— The angel said that the baby's Father
would be Jehovah God. That is
why Jesus would be called the
Son of God.

How do you think Mary felt about
this?— Did she say, "I don't want to be
the mother of Jesus"? No, Mary was ready to
do what God wanted. But how could God's Son in heaven be
born as a baby on earth? How was Jesus' birth different from the
birth of all other babies? Do you know?—

Well, God made our first parents, Adam and Eve, so that they
could come together in a wonderful way. Afterward, a baby
could begin to grow inside his mother. People say that this is
a miracle! I'm sure you will agree.

Now God did something that was an even more wonderful
miracle. He took the life of his Son from heaven and put it
inside Mary. God had never done that before, and he has never
done it since. As a result of this miracle, Jesus began to grow
inside of Mary just as other babies grow inside of their mothers.
After that, Mary married Joseph.

When the time came for Jesus to be born, Mary and Joseph
were visiting the city of Bethlehem. But it was full of people.

There was not even a room for Mary and Joseph, so they had to stay in a place where animals were kept. There Mary gave birth, and Jesus was put in a manger, as you can see here. A manger is a place that holds feed for cows and other animals to eat.

Why is Jesus being put in a manger?

Exciting things happened on the night Jesus was born. Near Bethlehem, an angel appeared to some shepherds. He told them that Jesus was an important person. The angel said: 'Look! I am telling you good news that will make people happy. Today someone was born who will save the people.'—Luke 2:10, 11.

The angel told the shepherds that they could find Jesus in Bethlehem, lying in a manger. Then, suddenly, other angels in heaven joined the first angel in praising God. 'Glory to God,'

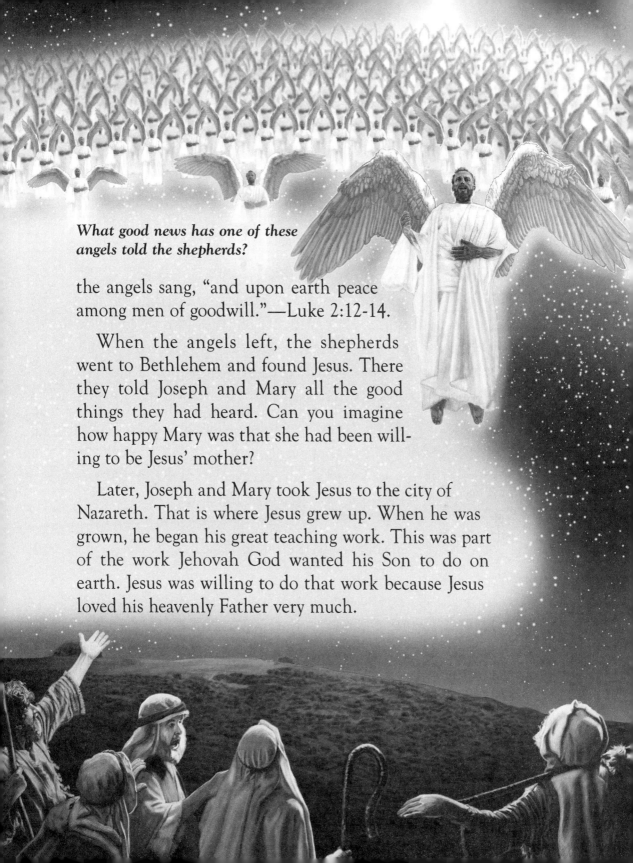

What good news has one of these angels told the shepherds?

the angels sang, "and upon earth peace among men of goodwill."—Luke 2:12-14.

When the angels left, the shepherds went to Bethlehem and found Jesus. There they told Joseph and Mary all the good things they had heard. Can you imagine how happy Mary was that she had been willing to be Jesus' mother?

Later, Joseph and Mary took Jesus to the city of Nazareth. That is where Jesus grew up. When he was grown, he began his great teaching work. This was part of the work Jehovah God wanted his Son to do on earth. Jesus was willing to do that work because Jesus loved his heavenly Father very much.

Before Jesus started his work as the Great Teacher, he was baptized in the Jordan River by John the Baptist. Then something amazing happened! As Jesus was coming up out of the water, Jehovah spoke from heaven, saying: "This is my Son, the beloved, whom I have approved." (Matthew 3:17) Don't you feel good when your parents tell you that they love you?— We can be sure that Jesus did too.

Jesus always did what was right. He did not pretend to be someone that he was not. He did not tell people that he was God. The angel Gabriel had told Mary that Jesus would be called the Son of God. Jesus himself said that he was God's Son. And he did not tell people that he knew more than his Father. He said: "The Father is greater than I am."—John 14:28.

Even in heaven, when Jesus' Father gave him work to do, Jesus did it. He did not say that he would do it but instead do something else. He loved his Father. So he listened to what his Father said. Then when Jesus came to the earth, he did what his heavenly Father sent him to do. He did not spend his time doing something else. No wonder that Jehovah is pleased with his Son!

We want to please Jehovah too, don't we?— Then we must show that we really listen to God, as Jesus did. God speaks to us through the Bible. It would not be right to pretend to listen to God but then to believe and do things that are contrary to the Bible, would it?— And remember, we will be happy to please Jehovah if we really love him.

Now read these other Bible texts that show what we need to know and believe about Jesus: Matthew 7:21-23; John 4:25, 26; and 1 Timothy 2:5, 6.

CHAPTER 6

THE GREAT TEACHER SERVED OTHER PEOPLE

DO YOU like it when someone does something nice for you?— Well, other people like it when someone does something nice for them too. We all do. The Great Teacher knew that, and he was always doing things for people. He said: 'I came, not to be served, but to serve.'—Matthew 20:28.

So if we want to be like the Great Teacher, what must we do?— We must serve others. We must do good things for them. It is true that many people do not do this. In fact, most people always want others to serve them. At one time even Jesus' followers felt this way. Each one wanted to be the greatest or the most important.

What were Jesus' followers arguing about?

One day Jesus was traveling with his disciples, who were his followers. After they entered the city of Capernaum, near the Sea of Galilee, they all went inside a house. There Jesus put the question to them: "What were you arguing over on the road?" They kept quiet because on the road they had argued among themselves about who was greater.—Mark 9:33, 34.

Jesus knew that it was not right for any one of his disciples to think that he was the greatest. So, as we learned in the first chapter of this book, he stood a small child in their midst and told them they should be humble like that little one. But still they did not learn. So shortly before he died, Jesus taught them a lesson that they would never forget. What did he do?—

Well, while they were all having a meal together, Jesus got up from the table and took off his outer garments. Picking up a towel, he wrapped it around his waist. Then he took a wash-basin and put water into it. His followers must have wondered what he was going to do. As they watched, Jesus went around to all of them, bent down, and washed their feet. Then he dried their feet with the towel. Just think of that! What if you had been there? How would you have felt?—

His followers did not feel that it was right for the Great Teacher to serve them in this way. They felt embarrassed. In fact, Peter was not going to let Jesus do this lowly service for him. But Jesus said that it was important for him to do it.

We do not usually wash one another's feet today. But this was done when Jesus was on earth. Do you know why?— Well, in the land where Jesus and his followers lived, people wore open sandals on their bare feet. So when they walked on the dirt roads, their feet got covered with dust. It was a kindness to wash the dust off the feet of a person who came into the house to visit.

But this time not one of Jesus' disciples had offered to wash the feet of the others. So Jesus did it himself. By doing this, Jesus taught his followers an important lesson. They needed to learn this lesson. And it is a lesson that we today need to learn.

Do you know what the lesson is?— After Jesus put his outer garments back on and took his place at the table again, he explained: "Do you know what I have done to you? You address me, 'Teacher,' and, 'Lord,' and you speak rightly, for I am such. Therefore, if I, although Lord and Teacher, washed your feet, you also ought to wash the feet of one another."—John 13:2-14.

Here the Great Teacher showed that he wanted his followers to serve one another. He did not want them to think only about themselves. He did not want them to think that they were so important that others should always serve them. He wanted them to be willing to serve others.

Wasn't that a fine lesson?— Will you be like the Great Teacher and serve other people?— We can all do things for others. This will make them happy. But best of all, it will make Jesus and his Father happy.

It is not hard to serve other people. If you watch, you will see many things that you can do for others. Think now: Is there

What lesson was Jesus teaching his followers?

anything that you can do to help your mother? You know that she does many things for you and the rest of the family. Can you help her?— Why not ask her?

Maybe you can set the table before the family eats. Or maybe you can clear the table of the dirty dishes after the family finishes eating. Some children take the garbage out every day. Whatever it is that you can do, you will be serving others, even as Jesus did.

Do you have younger brothers and sisters whom you can serve? Remember, Jesus, the Great Teacher, served even his followers. By serving your younger brothers and sisters, you will be copying Jesus. What can you do for them?— Maybe you can help them learn to put their toys away when they are finished playing.

What can you do to help others?

Or maybe you can help them get dressed. Or perhaps you can help them make their bed. Can you think of anything else you can do for them?— They will love you for doing these things, just as Jesus' followers loved him.

In school too you can serve other people. It might be your classmates or your teacher. If someone drops his books, it would be kind of you to help him pick them up. You might offer to clean the blackboard or to do something else for your teacher. Even holding the door open for someone is a kind service.

At times, we will find that people will not thank us for serving them. Do you think that this should stop us from doing good?— No! Many people did not thank Jesus for his good works. But that did not stop him from doing good.

So let's never hold back from serving other people. Let's remember the Great Teacher, Jesus, and always try to follow his example.

For more scriptures about helping other people, read Proverbs 3:27, 28; Romans 15:1, 2; and Galatians 6:2.

CHAPTER 7

OBEDIENCE PROTECTS YOU

WOULD you like it if you could do anything you wanted? Are there times when you wish that no one would ever tell you what to do? Now, be honest, and tell me what you think.—

But which is better for you? Is it really wise to do anything you want? Or do things turn out better when you obey your father and your mother?— God says that you should obey your parents, so there must be a good reason to do that. Let's see if we can figure it out.

How old are you?— Do you know how old your father is?— How old is your mother or your grandmother or grandfather?— They have lived much longer than you have. And the longer a person lives, the more time he has to learn things. He hears more things and sees more things and does more things every year. So young people can learn from older ones.

Why should you listen to older people?

Do you know someone who is younger than you are?— Do you know more than he or she does?— Why is it that you do?— It is because you have lived longer. You have had more time to learn things than someone younger has.

Who has lived longer than you or I or any other person?—Jehovah God has. He knows more than you do, and he knows more than I do. When he tells us to do anything, we can be sure that it is the right thing to do, even though it may be hard to do. Did you know that even the Great Teacher once found it hard to obey?—

One time God asked Jesus to do something very difficult. Jesus prayed about it, as we see here. He prayed: "If you wish, remove this cup from me." By praying this, Jesus showed that it was not always easy to do God's will. But how did Jesus finish his prayer? Do you know?—

Jesus finished it by saying: "Let, not my will, but yours take place." (Luke 22:41, 42) Yes, he wanted God's will to be done, not his own. And he went ahead and did what God wanted rather than what he thought would be best.

What can we learn from this?— We learn that it is always right to do what God says, even though it may not be easy to do. But we learn something else. Do you know what it is?— We learn that God and Jesus are not the same person, as some people say. Jehovah God is older and knows more than his Son, Jesus, does.

What can we learn from Jesus' prayer?

When we obey God, we are showing that we love him. The Bible says: "This is what the love of God means, that we observe his commandments." (1 John 5:3) So you see, we all need to obey God. You want to obey him, don't you?—

43

Let's get out our Bible and see what God tells children to do. We are going to read what the Bible says at Ephesians chapter 6, verses 1, 2, and 3. It says: "Children, be obedient to your parents in union with the Lord, for this is righteous: 'Honor your father and your mother'; which is the first command with a promise: 'That it may go well with you and you may endure a long time on the earth.'"

So you see, it is Jehovah God himself who is telling you to be obedient to your father and mother. What does it mean to "honor" them? It means that you are to show them respect. And God promises that if you obey your parents, it will "go well with you."

Let me tell you a story about some people whose lives were saved because they were obedient. These people lived long ago in the big city of Jerusalem. Most of the people in that city did not listen to God, so Jesus warned them that God was going to have their city destroyed. Jesus also told them how they could escape if they loved what was right. He said: 'When you see armies all around Jerusalem, you will know that its destruction is getting near. Then is the time to get out of Jerusalem and run to the mountains.'—Luke 21:20-22.

Well, just as Jesus said, armies came to attack Jerusalem. The armies of Rome camped all around it. Then, for some reason, the soldiers left. Most of the people thought that the danger had passed. So they stayed in the city. But what had Jesus said they should do?— What would you have done if you had been living in Jerusalem?— Those who really believed Jesus left their homes and ran to the mountains far away from Jerusalem.

*How did obedience
to Jesus' command
save these people?*

For a whole year, nothing happened to Jerusalem. In the second
year, nothing happened. And in the
third year, nothing happened. Some
people may have thought that those who
had left the city were foolish. But then in the fourth year, the
Roman armies came back. Again they camped all around Jerusalem. Now it was too late to escape. This time the armies
destroyed the city. Most of the people inside it died, and the rest
were taken prisoner.

But what happened to those who had obeyed Jesus?— They
were safe. They were far away from Jerusalem. So they were not
hurt. Obedience protected them.

If you are obedient, will that protect you too?— Your parents
may tell you never to play in the street. Why do they say that?—

45

Why should you obey
when you do not see any danger?

It is because you could be hit by a car. But someday you might think: 'There are no cars right now. I won't get hurt. Other children play in the street, and I have never seen them get hurt.'

That is how most of the people in Jerusalem felt. After the Roman armies left, it looked safe. Others were staying in the city. So they stayed too. They had been warned, but they did not listen. As a result, they lost their lives.

Let's take another example. Have you ever played with matches?— It may seem like fun to watch the fire when you light a match. But playing with matches can be dangerous. The whole house could burn down, and you could die!

Remember, obeying just some of the time is not enough. But if you always obey, that will really protect you. And who is it that tells you, "Children, be obedient to your parents"?— It is God. And, remember, he says that because he loves you.

Now read these scriptures that show the importance of obedience: Proverbs 23:22; Ecclesiastes 12:13; Isaiah 48:17, 18; and Colossians 3:20.

46

CHAPTER 8

OTHERS ARE HIGHER THAN WE ARE

I AM sure you will agree that others are higher, or greater and stronger, than you and I. Who would you say is?— Jehovah God is. What about his Son, the Great Teacher? Is he higher than we are?— Of course, he is.

Jesus had lived with God in heaven. He was a spirit Son, or angel. Did God make other angels, or spirit sons?— Yes, he made many millions of them. These angels also are higher and more powerful than we are.—Psalm 104:4; Daniel 7:10.

Do you remember the name of the angel who spoke to Mary?— It was Gabriel. He told Mary that her baby would be God's Son. God put the life of his spirit Son inside of Mary so that Jesus could be born as a baby on earth.—Luke 1:26, 27.

Do you believe that miracle? Do you believe that Jesus had lived with God in heaven?— Jesus said that he had. How did Jesus know about such things? Well, when he was a boy, Mary probably told him what Gabriel had said. Also, Joseph likely told Jesus that God was his real Father.

When Jesus was baptized, God even spoke from heaven, saying: "This is my Son." (Matthew 3:17) And the night before he died,

What did Mary and Joseph probably tell Jesus?

47

Jesus prayed: "Father, glorify me alongside yourself with the glory that I had alongside you before the world was." (John 17:5) Yes, Jesus asked to be taken back to live again with God in heaven. How could he live there?— Only if Jehovah God again made him an invisible spirit person, or angel.

Now I want to ask you an important question. Are all angels good? What do you think?— Well, at one time all of them were good. This was because Jehovah had created them, and everything he makes is good. But then one of the angels became bad. How did that happen?

To get the answer, we must go back to the time when God made the first man and woman, Adam and Eve. Some people say that the story about them is only make-believe. But the Great Teacher knew that it was true.

How could Adam and Eve have lived forever in Paradise?

When God made Adam and Eve, he put them in a beautiful garden in a place called Eden. It was a park, a paradise. They could have had a lot of children, a big family, and lived in Paradise forever. But there was an important lesson that they needed to learn. It's one we have already talked about. Let's see if we remember it.

Jehovah told Adam and Eve that they could eat all the fruit they wanted from the trees in the garden. But there was one tree they were not to eat from. God told them what would happen if they did. He said: "You will positively die." (Genesis 2:17) So, what was the lesson that Adam and Eve needed to learn?—

It was the lesson of obedience. Yes, life depends on obedience to Jehovah God! It was not enough for Adam and Eve just to say that they would obey him. They had to show that they would by the things they did. If they obeyed God, they would be showing that they loved him and wanted him to be their Ruler. Then they could have lived forever in Paradise. But if they ate from that tree, what would it show?—

It would show that they were not really thankful for what God had given them. Would you have obeyed Jehovah if you had been there?— At first, Adam and Eve did. But then someone higher than they were fooled Eve. He got her to disobey Jehovah. Who was that?—

Who was making the serpent speak to Eve?

The Bible says that a serpent, or snake, spoke to Eve. But you know that a serpent cannot speak all by itself. So how was it able to talk?— An angel made it seem like the serpent was speaking. But it was really the angel who was speaking. The angel had begun to think bad things. He wanted Adam and Eve to worship him. He wanted them to do the things that he said. He wanted to take God's place.

So that bad angel put wrong ideas into the mind of Eve. Through the serpent, he said to her: 'God did not tell you the truth. You will not die if you eat from that tree. You will become wise like God.' Would you have believed what that voice said?—

Eve began to want something that God had not given her. She ate fruit from the forbidden tree. Then she gave some to Adam. Adam did not believe what the serpent said. But his desire to be with Eve was stronger than his love for God. So he ate from the tree too.—Genesis 3:1-6; 1 Timothy 2:14.

What was the result?— Adam and Eve became imperfect, grew old, and died.

What happened to Adam and Eve after they disobeyed God?

And because they were imperfect, all their children were imperfect too and eventually grew old and died. God had not lied! Life does depend on obedience to him. (Romans 5:12) The Bible tells us that the angel who lied to Eve is called Satan the Devil, and other angels who became bad are called demons. —James 2:19; Revelation 12:9.

Now, can you understand why the good angel God had made became bad?— It was because he began to think bad things. He wanted to be Number One. He knew that God had told Adam and Eve to have children, and he wanted all of them to worship him. The Devil wants to make everyone disobey Jehovah. So he tries to put bad ideas into our minds.—James 1:13-15.

The Devil says that nobody really loves Jehovah. He says that you and I don't love God and that we don't really want to do what God says. He says that we obey Jehovah only when everything goes the way we like it. Is the Devil right? Are we like that?

The Great Teacher said that the Devil is a liar! Jesus proved that he really loved Jehovah by obeying Him. And Jesus did not obey God only when it was easy. He did it all the time, even when other people made it hard for him. He proved true to Jehovah right down till his death. That is why God brought him back to life to live forever.

So who would you say is our greatest enemy?— Yes, it is Satan the Devil. Can you see him?— Of course not! But we know that he exists and that he is higher and more powerful than we are. Yet, who is higher than the Devil?— Jehovah God is. So we know that God can protect us.

Read about the One we should worship: Deuteronomy 30:19, 20; Joshua 24:14, 15; Proverbs 27:11; and Matthew 4:10.

CHAPTER 9

WE NEED TO RESIST TEMPTATIONS

DID anyone ever ask you to do something that was wrong?— Did he dare you to do it? Or did he say that it would be fun and that it would not really be wrong to do it?— When someone does this to us, he is trying to tempt us.

What should we do when we are tempted? Should we give in and do what is wrong?— That would not please Jehovah God. But do you know who would be happy?— Yes, Satan the Devil would be.

Satan is the enemy of God, and Satan is our enemy. We cannot see him because he is a spirit. But he can see us. One day the Devil talked with Jesus, the Great Teacher, and tried to tempt him. Let's find out what Jesus did. Then we will know the right thing to do when we are tempted.

Jesus always wanted to do God's will. He openly showed this by being baptized in the Jordan River. It was right after Jesus' baptism that Satan tried to tempt Him. The Bible says that *"the heavens were opened up"* to Jesus. (Matthew 3:16) This could mean that Jesus now began to remember all about his earlier life in heaven with God.

What may Jesus have begun to remember when he was baptized?

After his baptism Jesus went into a wilderness to think about the things that he had begun to remember. Forty days and nights went by. All this time Jesus did not eat anything, so he was now very hungry. It was at this moment Satan tried to tempt Jesus.

The Devil said: "If you are a son of God, tell these stones to become loaves of bread." How good some bread would have tasted! But could Jesus have turned stones into loaves of bread?— Yes, he could have. Why? Because Jesus, the Son of God, had special powers.

Would you have made a stone into a loaf of bread if the Devil had asked you to do it?— Jesus was hungry. So wouldn't it have been all right to do it just once?— Jesus knew that it was wrong to use his powers in that way. Jehovah had given him those powers to draw people to God, not to use for himself.

So, instead, Jesus told Satan what is written in the Bible: 'Man must live, not on bread alone, but on every word that comes forth from Jehovah's mouth.' Jesus knew that doing what pleases Jehovah is even more important than having food to eat.

But the Devil tried again. He took Jesus into Jerusalem and had him stand

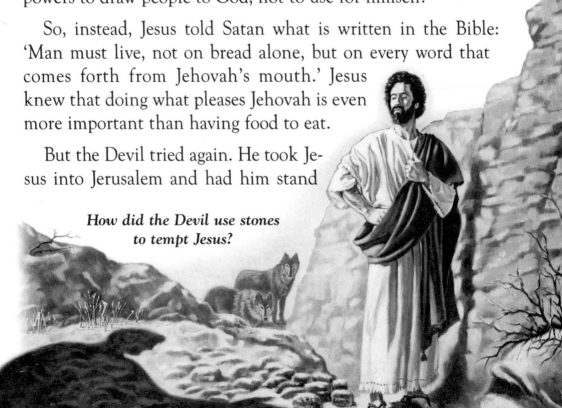

How did the Devil use stones to tempt Jesus?

up on a high part of the temple. Then Satan said: 'If you are a son of God, throw yourself down from here. For it is written that God's angels will keep you from hurting yourself.'

Why did Satan say this?— He said it to tempt Jesus to do something foolish. But again Jesus did not listen to Satan. He told Satan: "It is written, 'You must not put Jehovah your God to the test.'" Jesus knew that it was wrong to test Jehovah by taking chances with his life.

Still, Satan did not give up. Next he took Jesus along to a very high mountain. There he showed him all the kingdoms, or governments, of the world and their glory. Then Satan said to Jesus: "All these things I will give you if you fall down and do an act of worship to me."

Think about the Devil's offer. Did all these kingdoms, or governments of men, really belong to Satan?— Well, Jesus did not deny that they were Satan's. He would have done that if Satan had not owned them. Yes, Satan really is the ruler of all the nations of the world. The Bible even calls him "the ruler of this world."—John 12:31.

What would you do if the Devil promised you something if you worshiped him?— Jesus knew that it would be wrong to worship the Devil no matter what He would get. So Jesus said: 'Go away, Satan! For the Bible says that it is Jehovah your God you must worship and that you must serve only him.'—Matthew 4:1-10; Luke 4:1-13.

We also are faced with temptations. Do you know of some of them?— Here is an example. Your mother may make a delicious pie or cake for dessert. She may tell you not to eat any of it until mealtime. But you are very hungry, so you may feel tempted

Why could Satan offer Jesus all these kingdoms?

to eat it. Will you obey your mother?— Satan wants you to disobey her.

Remember Jesus. He was very hungry too. But he knew that pleasing God was more important than eating. You show that you are like Jesus when you do what your mother says.

It may be that other children will ask you to swallow some pills. They may tell you that these will make you feel really good. But these

What will you do if you are tempted?

pills may be drugs. They can make you very sick and can even kill you. Or someone may give you a cigarette, which also contains drugs, and dare you to smoke it. What will you do?—

Remember Jesus. Satan tried to get Jesus to take chances with his life by telling him to jump off the temple. But Jesus would not do it. What will you do if someone dares you to do something dangerous?— Jesus did not listen to Satan. Neither should you listen to anyone who tries to get you to do wrong things.

Someday you may be asked to do an act of worship to an image, something that the Bible says we must not do. (Exodus 20: 4, 5) It may be part of a ceremony at school. You may be told that you cannot even go to school anymore if you refuse to do this. What will you do?—

It is easy to do what is right when everyone else is. But doing what is right can be pretty hard when others are trying to get us to do wrong. They may say that what they are doing is not really so bad. But the big question is, What does God say about it? He knows best.

So no matter what others say, we should never do things that God says are wrong. In that way we will always make God happy, and we will never please the Devil.

More information about how to resist temptations to do wrong can be found at Psalm 1:1, 2; Proverbs 1:10, 11; Matthew 26:41; and 2 Timothy 2:22.

Why is it wrong to use images in worship?

CHAPTER 10

JESUS' POWER OVER THE DEMONS

DO YOU remember why one of God's angels became Satan the Devil?— It was his selfish desire to be worshiped that caused him to turn against God. Did other angels become followers of Satan?— Yes, they did. The Bible calls them 'Satan's angels,' or demons.—Revelation 12:9.

Do these bad angels, or demons, believe in God?— 'The demons believe God exists,' the Bible says. (James 2:19) But now they are afraid. This is because they know that God will punish them for the bad things they have done. What have they done wrong?—

The Bible says that those angels left their own proper home in heaven and came to earth to live as men. They did this because they wanted to have sex relations with the pretty women on earth. (Genesis 6:1, 2; Jude 6) What do you know about sex relations?—

What did these angels do that was bad?

Sex relations are when a man and a woman become close in a very special way. Afterward, a baby can grow inside the mother. But for angels to have sex relations is wrong. God wants only a man and a woman who are married to each other to have sex relations. That way if a baby is born, the husband and wife can take care of it.

When angels took human bodies and had sex with women on earth, their babies grew up to become giants. They were very mean, and they would hurt people. So God brought a great flood to destroy the giants and all the bad people. But he had Noah build an ark, or big boat, to save the few people who did what was right. The Great Teacher said that what happened at the Flood is important to remember.—Genesis 6:3, 4, 13, 14; Luke 17: 26, 27.

When the Flood came, do you know what happened to the bad angels?— They stopped using the human bodies they had made, and they went back to heaven. But they could no longer be God's angels, so they

Why is there more trouble on earth now than ever before?

became angels of Satan, or demons. And what happened to their children, the giants?— They died in the Flood. And so did all the other people who did not obey God.

Since the time of the Flood, God has not let the demons become like humans anymore. But even though we cannot see them, the demons still try to get people to do very bad things. They are causing more trouble than ever before. This is because they have been thrown out of heaven down to the earth.

Do you know why we cannot see the demons?— It is because they are invisible. But we can be sure that they are alive. The Bible says that Satan is 'misleading people in all the world,' and his demons are helping him.—Revelation 12:9, 12.

Can the Devil and his demons mislead, or fool, us too?— Yes, they can if we are not careful. But we do not need to be afraid. The Great Teacher said: 'The Devil has no hold on me.' If we keep close to God, he will protect us from the Devil and his demons.—John 14:30.

It is important that we know what bad things the demons will try to get us to do. So think about it. What bad things did the demons do when they came to earth?— Before the Flood, they had sex relations with women, something that was not right for angels to do. Today the demons like it when people do not obey God's law about sex relations. Let me ask you, Who only should have sex relations?— You are right, only married people.

Today some young boys and girls have sex relations, but this is wrong for them. The Bible talks about the male "genital organ," or penis. (Leviticus 15:1-3) The female genital parts are called the vulva. Jehovah created these parts of the body for a special purpose that should be enjoyed only by married people. It makes the demons happy when people do things that are forbidden by Jehovah. For example, the demons like it when a boy and a girl play with each other's penis or vulva. We don't want to make the demons happy, do we?—

There is something else that the demons like but Jehovah hates. Do you know what it is?— Violence. (Psalm 11:5) Violence is when people are mean and hurt others. Remember, that is what the giants, the sons of the demons, did.

The demons also like to scare people. Sometimes they pretend to be people who have died. They may even imitate voices of those who have died. In this way the demons fool many into believing that dead

What can happen if we watch violence?

people are alive and can talk with the living. Yes, the demons cause many people to believe in ghosts.

60

So we must be on guard that Satan and his demons do not fool us. The Bible warns: 'Satan tries to make himself look like a good angel, and his servants do the same.' (2 Corinthians 11: 14, 15) But, really, the demons are bad. Let's see how they may try to get us to be like them.

Where do people learn a lot about violence and improper sex and spirits and ghosts?— Isn't it from watching certain television shows and movies, playing computer and video games, going on the Internet, and reading comic books? Does doing these things bring us closer to God or closer to the Devil and his demons? What do you think?—

What is it good for us to do?

Who do you think wants us to listen to and watch bad things?— Yes, Satan and his demons do. So, what do you and I need to do?— We need to read, listen to, and watch things that are good for us and that will help us to serve Jehovah. Can you think of some of these good things that we can do?—

If we do what is good, there is no reason to be afraid of the demons. Jesus is stronger than they are, and they are afraid of him. One day the demons cried out to Jesus: "Did you come to destroy us?" (Mark 1:24) Won't we be happy when the time comes for Jesus to destroy Satan and his demons?— In the meantime, we can be sure that Jesus will protect us from the demons if we keep close to him and his heavenly Father.

Let's read about what we need to do, at 1 Peter 5:8, 9 and James 4:7, 8.

CHAPTER 11

HELP FROM GOD'S ANGELS

SOME people say that they believe only what they can see. But that is foolish. There are lots of real things that we have never seen with our eyes. Can you name one?—

What about the air we breathe? Can we feel it?— Hold up your hand, and blow on it. Did you feel anything?— You did, but you can't see the air, can you?—

We have already talked about spirit persons, whom we can't see. We learned that some are good but others are bad. Name some good spirit persons whom we cannot see.— Yes, there is Jehovah God, there is Jesus, and there are good angels. Are there also bad angels?— The Bible says there are. Tell me what you have learned about them.—

One thing we know is that both good angels and bad ones are stronger than we are. The Great Teacher knew a lot about angels. That was because he had been an angel before he was born as a baby on earth. He had lived with other angels in heaven. He knew millions of them. Do all these angels have names?—

Well, we learned that God gave names to the stars. So we can be sure that all the angels have names too. And we know that they can speak to one another because the Bible tells about the 'language of angels.' (1 Corinthians 13:1) What do you think angels talk about? Do they talk about us on earth?—

We know that Satan's angels, the demons, are trying to get us to disobey Jehovah. So they must talk about how they can do this. They want us to be like them so that Jehovah won't like us either. But what about God's faithful angels? Do you think that they also talk about us?— Yes, they do. They want to help us. Let me tell you how some of God's angels helped people who loved Jehovah and served him.

For example, there was the man named Daniel who lived in Babylon. Many people there did not love Jehovah. People even made a law that would punish anyone who prayed to Jehovah God. But Daniel would not stop praying to Jehovah. Do you know what they did to Daniel?—

Yes, bad people had Daniel thrown into a lions' den. There Daniel was all alone with some

What did God do to save Daniel?

hungry lions. Do you know what happened then?— "God sent his angel and shut the mouth of the lions," Daniel said. He was not hurt at all! Angels can do wonderful things for those who serve Jehovah.—Daniel 6:18-22.

Then there was the time Peter was in prison. You will remember that Peter was a friend of the Great Teacher, Jesus Christ. Some people did not like it when Peter told them that Jesus was the Son of God. So they put Peter in prison. Soldiers were guarding Peter to make sure that he didn't get away. Was there anyone who could help him?—

Peter was sleeping between two guards, and there were chains on his hands. But the Bible says: 'Look! Jehovah's an-

How did an angel help Peter get out of prison?

gel came, and a light began to shine in the prison cell. Touching Peter on his side, the angel woke him, saying, "Rise quickly!"'

At that, Peter's chains fell off his hands! And the angel said to him: 'Get dressed, put your sandals on, and follow me.' The guards couldn't stop them because the angel was helping Peter. Now they came to an iron gate, and a strange thing happened. The gate opened by itself! That angel had set Peter free so that he could keep on preaching.—Acts 12:3-11.

Can God's angels help us too?— Yes, they can. Does this mean that they will never let us get hurt at all?— No, angels do not stop us from getting hurt if we do foolish things. But even if we don't do foolish things, we may still get hurt. The angels are not told to keep this from happening. Instead, God has given them special work to do.

The Bible talks about an angel who tells people everywhere to worship God. (Revelation 14:6, 7) How does the angel tell them that? Does he shout from heaven so that everyone can hear him?— No, rather, Jesus' followers on earth talk to others about God, and the angels guide them in their work. The angels make sure that those who really want to know about God have a chance to hear. We can share in that preaching work, and the angels will help us.

But what if people who do not love God make trouble for us? What if they put us in prison? Would the angels set us free?— They could. But that is not what they always do.

Jesus' follower Paul was once a prisoner. He was traveling on a boat during a bad storm. But the angels did not set him free right away. This was because there were other people who needed to hear about God. An angel said: "Have no fear, Paul. You must stand before Caesar." Yes, Paul was to be taken to the world ruler Caesar so that Paul could preach to him. The angels always knew where Paul was, and they helped him. They will help us too if we really serve God.—Acts 27:23-25.

There is another big work that the angels will do, and they are going to do it soon. God's time to destroy wicked people is very near. All who do not worship the true God will be destroyed. Those who say they do not believe in angels because they cannot see them will find out how wrong they are. —2 Thessalonians 1:6-8.

What will that mean for us?— If we are on the same side with God's angels, they will help us. But are we on their side?— We are if we serve Jehovah. And if we serve Jehovah, we will be telling other people to serve him too.

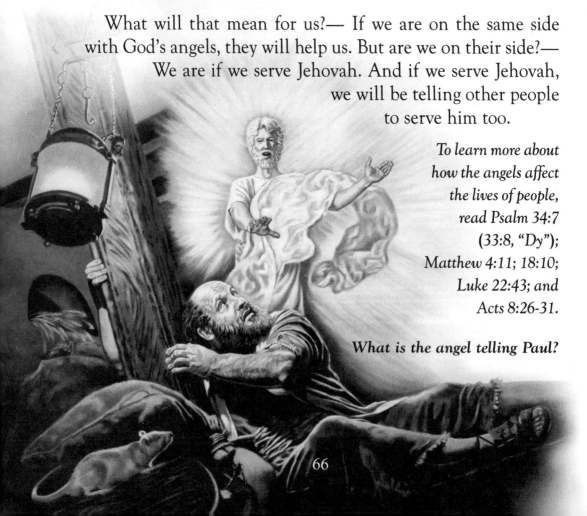

To learn more about how the angels affect the lives of people, read Psalm 34:7 (33:8, "Dy"); Matthew 4:11; 18:10; Luke 22:43; and Acts 8:26-31.

What is the angel telling Paul?

CHAPTER 12

JESUS TEACHES US TO PRAY

DO YOU talk to Jehovah God?— He wants you to talk to him. When you talk to God, this is called prayer. Jesus often spoke to his Father in heaven. Sometimes he wanted to be alone when he talked to God. One time, the Bible says, "He went up into the mountain by himself to pray. Though it became late, he was there alone."—Matthew 14:23.

Where can you go to pray alone to Jehovah?— Maybe you can be alone to talk to Jehovah before you go to bed at night. Jesus said: "When you pray, go into your private room and, after shutting your door, pray to your Father." (Matthew 6:6) Do you pray to Jehovah each night before you go to sleep?— You should do so.

Jesus also prayed when other people were with him. When his friend Lazarus died, Jesus prayed with

Jesus prayed when he was alone . . . and when he was with others

others at the place where Lazarus had been laid. (John 11:41, 42) And Jesus would also pray when he had meetings with his disciples. Do you go to meetings where prayer is said?— There an older person will usually pray. Listen carefully to what he says because he is talking to God for you. Then you will be able to say "Amen" to the prayer. Do you know what it means to say "Amen" at the end of a prayer?— It means that you like the prayer. It means that you agree with it and that you want it to be your prayer too.

Jesus also prayed at mealtimes. He thanked Jehovah for his food. Do you always pray before you eat your meals?— It is good for us to thank Jehovah for the food before we start eating. Someone else may say the prayer when you eat together. But what if you eat by yourself? Or what if you have a meal with people who do not thank Jehovah?— Then you need to say your own prayer.

Do you always have to pray out loud? Or can Jehovah hear you if you say your prayer to yourself?— We can learn the answer from what happened to Nehemiah. He was a worshiper of

Jehovah who worked in the palace of Persian King Artaxerxes. One day Nehemiah became very sad because he heard that the walls of Jerusalem, the main city of his people, were broken down.

When the king asked Nehemiah why he was sad, Nehemiah first said a silent prayer. Then Nehemiah told the king why he was sad and asked him if he could go to Jerusalem to rebuild the walls. What happened?—

Yes, God answered Nehemiah's prayer. The king said that he could go! The king even gave Nehemiah a lot of trees to use to build the walls. So God really can answer our prayers, even when they are silent.—Nehemiah 1:2, 3; 2:4-8.

Now think about this. Should you bow your head when you

When can you say a silent prayer, as Nehemiah did?

pray? Should you get down on your knees? What do you think?— Sometimes Jesus got down on his knees when he prayed. Other times he stood up. And at times he lifted his head toward heaven as he prayed, as he did when he prayed for Lazarus.

So, what does this show?— Yes, this shows that the position you are in is not the important thing. Sometimes it is good to bow your head and close your eyes. At other times you may even want to get down on your knees, as Jesus did. But, remember, we can pray to God at any time during the day or night, and he will hear us. The important thing about prayer is that we really believe that Jehovah is listening. Do you believe that Jehovah hears your prayers?—

What should we say in our prayers to Jehovah?— Tell me: When you pray, what do you talk to God about?— Jehovah gives us so many good things, and it is right to thank him for them, isn't it?— We can thank him for the food we eat. But have you ever thanked him for the blue sky, the green trees, and the pretty flowers?— He made those too.

Jesus' disciples once asked him to teach them how to pray. So the Great Teacher did, and he showed them what were the most important things to pray for. Do you know what these

What can you talk to God about in prayer?

70

things are?— Get your Bible, and open it to Matthew chapter 6. In verses 9 through 13, we find what many people call the Our Father or the Lord's Prayer. Let's read it together.

Here we learn that Jesus told us to pray about God's name. He said to pray that God's name be sanctified, or treated as holy. What is God's name?— Yes, it is Jehovah, and we should love that name.

Second, Jesus taught us to pray for God's Kingdom to come. This Kingdom is important because it will bring peace to the earth and make it a paradise.

Third, the Great Teacher said to pray for God's will to be done on earth just as it is done in heaven. If we pray for this, then we should do what God wants.

Next, Jesus taught us to pray for the food we need for the day. He also said that we should tell God we are sorry when we have done things that are wrong. And we should ask God to forgive us. But before he will do so, we must forgive others if they have done something wrong to us. Is that easy for you to do?—

Finally, Jesus said we should pray that Jehovah God will protect us from the wicked one, Satan the Devil. So all of these are good things to pray to God about.

We should believe that Jehovah hears our prayers. Besides asking him to help us, we should keep thanking him. He is happy when we mean what we say in prayer and when we ask him for the right things. And he will give us these things. Do you believe that?—

More good counsel about prayer is found at Romans 12:12; 1 Peter 3:12; and 1 John 5:14.

CHAPTER 13

THOSE WHO BECAME JESUS' DISCIPLES

WHO is the finest servant of God that ever lived?— That's right, Jesus Christ. Do you think that we can be like him?— Well, the Bible says that he set the example for us to follow. And he invites us to be his disciples.

Do you know what it means to be a disciple of Jesus?— It means several things. First, we must learn from him. But that is not all. We must also really believe what he says. If we do, we will do what he tells us.

Many people say that they believe in Jesus. Do you think all of them are really his disciples?— No, most of them are not. They may go to church. But many of them have never taken time to learn what Jesus taught. Really, only those who follow Jesus' example are his disciples.

Let's talk about some of those who were Jesus' disciples when he was a man on earth. One of the first to become a disciple is Philip. Philip goes to find his friend Nathanael (also called Bartholomew), whom you see sitting under a tree. When Nathanael comes to Jesus, Jesus says: 'See, here is an honest man, a true son of Israel.' Nathanael is surprised and asks: 'How do you know me?'

Who is this man, and how does he become a disciple of Jesus?

"Before Philip called you, while you were under the fig tree, I saw you," Jesus says. Nathanael is amazed that Jesus knew exactly where he was, so Nathanael says: "You are the Son of God, you are King of Israel."—John 1:49.

Others became disciples of Jesus the day before Philip and Nathanael did.

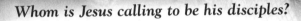

Whom is Jesus calling to be his disciples?

These are Andrew and his brother Peter as well as John and perhaps John's brother James. (John 1:35-51) After a while, however, these four go back to their fishing business. Then one day while Jesus is walking beside the Sea of Galilee, he sees Peter and Andrew letting down a fishing net into the sea. Jesus calls to them: "Come after me."

Going a little farther, Jesus sees James and John. They are in a boat with their father, fixing their fishing nets. Jesus calls them to follow him too. What would you have done if Jesus had called you? Would you have gone with him right away?— These men know who Jesus is. They know that he has been sent by God. So at once they leave their fishing business and follow Jesus.—Matthew 4:18-22.

When these men became Jesus' followers, did it mean that afterward they always did what was right?— No. You may remember that these men even argued among themselves about which one of them was the greatest. But they listened to Jesus, and they were willing to change. If we are willing to change, we too can be disciples of Jesus.

Jesus invited all sorts of people to be his disciples. Once, a rich young ruler came to Jesus and asked how to gain everlasting life. When the rich ruler said that he had been obeying God's commandments from his childhood on, Jesus invited him: "Come be my follower." Do you know what happened?—

Well, when the man learned that being a disciple of Jesus had to be more important than being rich, he was very unhappy. He did not become Jesus' disciple because he loved his money more than he loved God.—Luke 18:18-25.

After Jesus had been preaching for nearly a year and a half, he chose 12 of his disciples to be apostles. The apostles were men whom he sent out to do special work. Do you know their names?— Let's see if we can learn them. Look at their pictures here, and see if you can say their names. Then try to say their names from memory.

Eventually, one of the 12 apostles became bad. He was Judas Iscariot. Afterward, another disciple was chosen to become

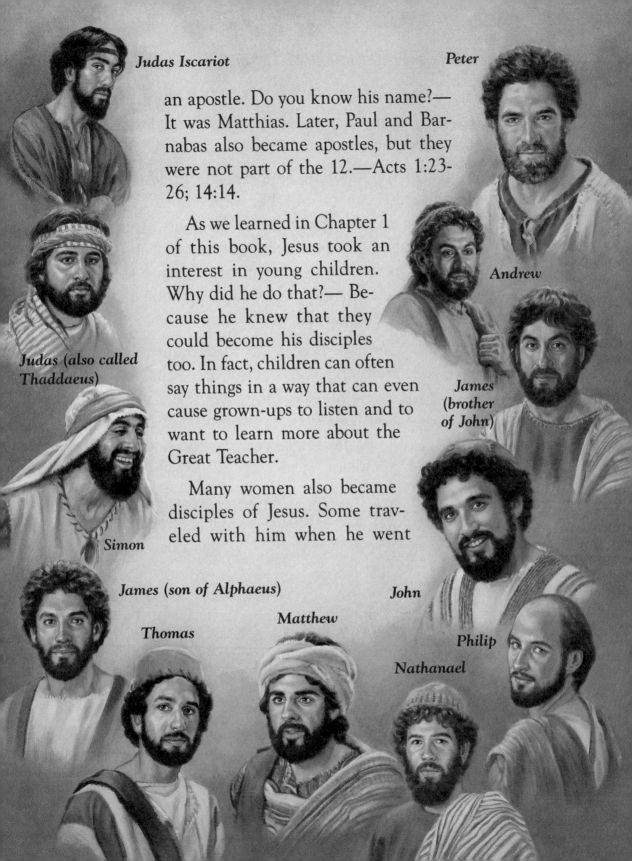

Judas Iscariot

Peter

an apostle. Do you know his name?—
It was Matthias. Later, Paul and Barnabas also became apostles, but they
were not part of the 12.—Acts 1:23-
26; 14:14.

As we learned in Chapter 1
of this book, Jesus took an
interest in young children.
Why did he do that?— Be-
cause he knew that they
could become his disciples
too. In fact, children can often
say things in a way that can even
cause grown-ups to listen and to
want to learn more about the
Great Teacher.

Many women also became
disciples of Jesus. Some traveled with him when he went

Andrew

James
(brother
of John)

Judas (also called
Thaddaeus)

Simon

James (son of Alphaeus)

John

Thomas

Matthew

Philip

Nathanael

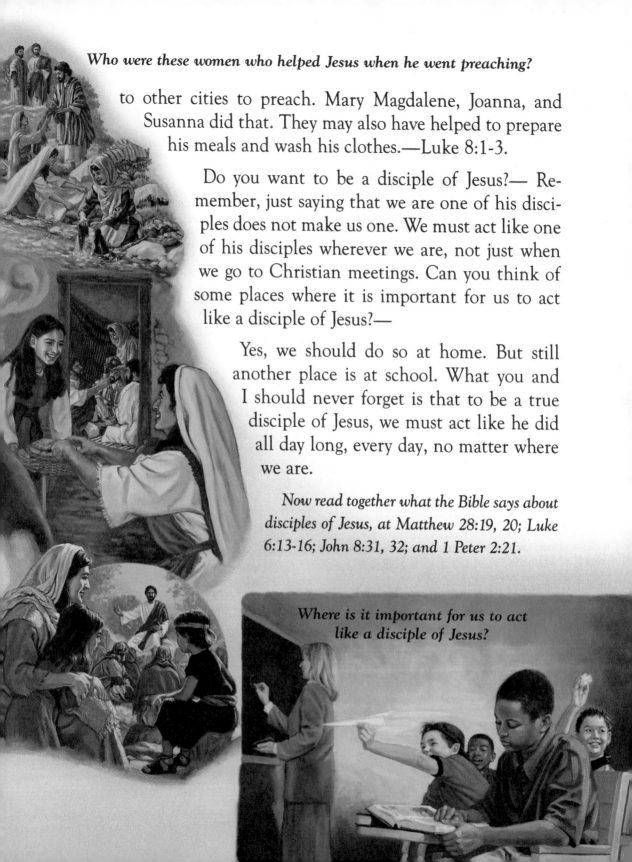

Who were these women who helped Jesus when he went preaching?

to other cities to preach. Mary Magdalene, Joanna, and Susanna did that. They may also have helped to prepare his meals and wash his clothes.—Luke 8:1-3.

Do you want to be a disciple of Jesus?— Remember, just saying that we are one of his disciples does not make us one. We must act like one of his disciples wherever we are, not just when we go to Christian meetings. Can you think of some places where it is important for us to act like a disciple of Jesus?—

Yes, we should do so at home. But still another place is at school. What you and I should never forget is that to be a true disciple of Jesus, we must act like he did all day long, every day, no matter where we are.

Now read together what the Bible says about disciples of Jesus, at Matthew 28:19, 20; Luke 6:13-16; John 8:31, 32; and 1 Peter 2:21.

Where is it important for us to act like a disciple of Jesus?

CHAPTER 14

WHY WE SHOULD FORGIVE

HAS anyone ever done something wrong to you?— Did he hurt you or say something unkind to you?— Should you treat him in the same unkind way that he treated you?—

If someone hurts them, many people will hurt that person to pay him back. But Jesus taught that we should forgive those who do wrong to us. (Matthew 6:12) What if a person is unkind to us many times? How many times should we forgive him?—

That is what Peter wanted to know. So one day he asked Jesus: 'Do I have to forgive him as many as seven times?' Seven times is not enough. Jesus said: 'You are to forgive seventy-seven times' if the person sins against you that many times.

That is a lot of times! We would not even remember that many wrongs or bad things that a person did to us, would we? And this is what Jesus was telling us: We should not try to remember the number of wrongs others may do to us. If they ask to be forgiven, we should forgive them.

Jesus wanted to show his disciples how very important it is to be forgiving. So after he answered Peter's

What did Peter want to know about forgiveness?

What happened when the slave begged the king for more time to pay?

question, he told his disciples a story. Would you like to hear it?—

Once there was a good king. He was very kind. He would even lend money to his slaves when they needed help. But the day came when the king wanted his slaves who owed him money to pay him back. Well, one slave was brought in who owed the king 60 million pieces of money. That's a lot of money!

How did the slave treat his fellow slave who could not pay him what he owed?

But the slave had spent all the king's money and could not pay the king back. So the king gave orders for him to be sold. The king also said to sell the slave's wife and his children and everything that he owned. Then, with the money received from the sale, the king was to be paid. How do you suppose this made the slave feel?—

He knelt down before the king and begged: 'Please, give me more time, and I will pay back everything that I owe you.' If you had been the king, what would you have done with the slave?— The king felt sorry for his slave. So the king forgave him. He told the slave that he did not have to pay back any of the money, not even one of the 60 million pieces. How happy that must have made the slave!

But what did that slave do then? He went out and found another slave, one who owed him just one hundred pieces of money. He grabbed this fellow slave by the neck and began to choke him, saying: 'Pay back the one hundred pieces you owe me!' Can you imagine a person doing something like that, especially after having been forgiven so much by the king?—

Well, the slave who owed just one hundred pieces of money was poor. He could not pay the money back right away. So he fell down at the feet of his fellow slave and begged: 'Please, give me more time, and I will pay back what I owe you.' Should the man have given his fellow slave more time?— What would you have done?—

This man was not kind, as the king had been. He wanted his money right away. And because his fellow slave could not pay it, he had him thrown into prison. Other slaves saw all of this happen, and they did not like it. They felt sorry for the slave who was in prison. So they went and told the king about it.

The king did not like what had happened either. He became very angry at the unforgiving slave. So he called him and said: 'You bad slave, didn't I forgive what you owed me? So should you not have been forgiving to your fellow slave?'

The unforgiving slave should have learned a lesson from the good king. But he had not. So now the king had that slave thrown into prison until he could pay back the 60 million pieces of money. And, of course, in jail he could never earn the money to pay the king back. So he would stay there till he died.

As Jesus finished telling this story, he said to his followers: "In like manner my heavenly Father will also deal with you if you do not forgive each one his brother from your hearts." —Matthew 18:21-35.

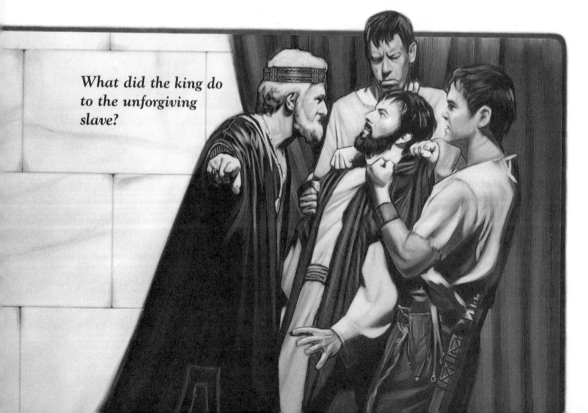

What did the king do to the unforgiving slave?

You see, we all owe God very much. In fact, our very life comes from God! So when compared with what we owe to God, other people owe us little. What they owe us is like the one hundred pieces of money that the one slave owed to the other. But what we owe to God because of the wrong things we do is like the 60 million pieces that the slave owed to the king.

God is very kind. Though we have done wrong things, he forgives us. He does not make us pay by taking our lives away from us forever. But this is the lesson we need to remember: *God forgives us only if we forgive people who do wrong to us.* That's something to think about, isn't it?—

So if someone does something unkind to you but then says that he is sorry, what will you do? Will you forgive him?— What if it happens many times? Will you still forgive him?—

If we were the person who is asking to be forgiven, we would want the other person to forgive us, wouldn't we?— So we should do the same for him. Not only should we say that we forgive him but we should really forgive him from our heart. When we do that, we show that we really want to be followers of the Great Teacher.

To understand the importance of being forgiving, let's also read Proverbs 19:11; Matthew 6:14, 15; and Luke 17:3, 4.

What will you do if someone asks you to forgive him?

CHAPTER 15

A LESSON ON BEING KIND

DO YOU know what prejudice is?— Well, prejudice is not liking someone simply because he may look different or may speak a different language. So being prejudiced is having a bad feeling or a belief about someone before you really get to know him.

Do you think it is right not to like someone before you really know what kind of person he is or just because he is different?— No, prejudice is not right, and neither is it kind. We should not be unkind to someone just because he may be different from us.

Think about it. Do you know anyone whose skin color is different from yours or who speaks a language different from yours?— Maybe you even know people who look different because they have been hurt or they have a sickness. Are you kind and loving to those who are different from you?—

If we listen to the Great Teacher, Jesus Christ, we will be kind to everyone. It should not make any difference to us what country a person may come from or what color his skin is. We should be kind to him. Although this is not what all people believe, it is a lesson Jesus taught. Let's talk about it.

A Jew who was prejudiced toward others came to Jesus and asked the question, 'What must I do to live forever?' Jesus knew that the man was probably trying to get him to say we should be kind only to people of our own race or nationality. So instead of answering the question himself, Jesus asked the man: 'What does God's Law say we must do?'

The man answered: 'You must love Jehovah your God with all your heart, and you must love your neighbor as yourself.' Jesus said: 'You answered right. Keep on doing this and you will get everlasting life.'

The man, however, did not want to be kind or loving to people who were different from him. So he tried to find an excuse. He asked Jesus: "Who really is my neighbor?" He may have wanted Jesus to say: "Your neighbors are your friends" or, "They are people who look the same as you do." To answer the question, Jesus told a story about a Jew and a Samaritan. This is how it went.

A man was going down the road from the city of Jerusalem to Jericho. This man was a Jew. As he was walking along, robbers grabbed him. They knocked him down and took his money and his clothes. The robbers beat him up and left him half dead beside the road.

How should we treat those who may be different from us?

A short time later, a priest came along that road. He saw the man who was badly hurt. What would you have done?— Well, the priest just went by on the opposite side of the road. He didn't even stop. He didn't do anything at all to help the man.

Then another very religious man came down the road. He was a Levite who served at the temple in Jerusalem. Would he stop to help?— No. He did the very same thing that the priest did.

Finally, a Samaritan came along. Can you see him coming around the bend in the road?— He saw the Jew lying there badly hurt. Now, most Samaritans and Jews did not like one another at all. (John 4:9) So would this Samaritan leave the man

84

without helping him? Would he say to himself: 'Why should I help this Jew? He would not help me if I was hurt'?

Well, the Samaritan looked at the man lying beside the road, and he felt sorry for him. He could not leave him there and let him die. So he got off his animal, went over to the man, and began caring for his wounds. He poured oil and wine upon them. This would help the wounds to heal. Then he wrapped up the wounds with a cloth.

The Samaritan gently lifted the hurt man onto his animal. Then they went slowly down the road until they came to an inn, or small hotel. There the Samaritan got a place for the man to stay, and he took good care of him.

Now Jesus asked the man he was talking to: 'Who of these three men do you think was the good neighbor?' What would you say? Was it the priest, the Levite, or the Samaritan?—

The man answered: 'The man who stopped and took care of the hurt man was the good neighbor.' Jesus said: 'You are right. Go your way and do the same yourself.' —Luke 10:25-37.

Why was the Samaritan the good neighbor?

How can you be a good neighbor?

Wasn't that a fine story? It makes clear who our neighbors are. They are not just our close friends. And they are not just people who have the same skin color as we do or speak the same language. Jesus taught us to be kind to people regardless of where they are from, what they look like, or what language they speak.

This is the way Jehovah God is. He is not prejudiced. 'Your Father who is in heaven makes his sun rise on bad people and good people,' Jesus said. 'And he makes the rain fall on good people and those who are not good.' So, then, we should be kind to all, just as God is.—Matthew 5:44-48.

So if you see someone hurt, what will you do?— What if the person is from a different country or his skin color is different from yours? He is still your neighbor, and you should help him. If you feel too small to help, then you can ask an older person for help. Or you can call a policeman or a schoolteacher. That is being kind, like the Samaritan man.

The Great Teacher wants us to be kind. He wants us to help others, no matter who they may be. That is why he told the story about the kind Samaritan.

On this lesson of being kind to people regardless of their race or nationality, read Proverbs 19:22; Acts 10:34, 35; and 17:26.

CHAPTER 16

WHAT IS TRULY IMPORTANT?

THERE was a man who came to see Jesus one day. He knew that Jesus was very wise, so he said to him: 'Teacher, tell my brother to give me some of the things he has.' The man thought he should have some of those things.

If you had been Jesus, what would you have said?— Jesus saw that the man had a problem. But the problem was not that he needed what his brother had. The man's problem was that he did not know what was truly important in life.

Let's think about this. What should be most important to us? Should it be having nice toys, new clothes, or things like that?— No, there is something that is much more important. And this is the lesson that Jesus wanted to teach. So he told a story about a man who forgot God. Would you like to hear it?—

What problem did this man have?

This man was very rich. He owned land and barns. The crops that he planted grew very well. He did not have room in his barns to store all the crops. So, what was he going to do? Well, he said to himself: 'I will tear down my barns and build bigger ones. Then I will store all my crops and all my good things in these new barns.'

The rich man thought that this was the wise thing to do. He

87

thought that he was very smart to store up many things. He said to himself: 'I have many good things stored up. They will last me for many years. So now I can take it easy. I will eat, drink, and enjoy myself.' But there was something wrong with the rich man's thinking. Do you know what it was?— He was thinking only about himself and his own pleasure. He forgot about God.

What is this rich man thinking about?

So God spoke to the rich man. He said: 'You foolish man. You are going to die tonight. Now who will have the things that you stored up?' Could that rich man use those things after he died?— No, someone else would get them. Jesus said: "So it goes with the man that lays up treasure for himself but is not rich toward God."—Luke 12:13-21.

You don't want to be like that rich man, do you?— His main purpose in life was the getting of material things. That was a mistake. He always wanted more. But he was not "rich toward God."

Many people are like that rich man. They always want more. But this can lead to big problems. For example, you have toys, don't you?— What are some of the toys that you have? Tell me.— What if one of your friends has a ball or a doll or some other toy that you don't have? Would it be right for you to try to make your parents buy one for you?—

There may be times when a toy seems very important. But what happens to it after a while?— It gets old. It may fall apart, and then you don't even want it anymore. Really, you have something that is much more precious than toys. Do you know what it is?—

What do you have that is more precious than toys?

It is your life. Your life is very important because without it, you can't do anything. But your life depends on doing what pleases God, doesn't it?— So let's not be like that foolish rich man who forgot God.

Children are not the only ones who may do foolish things like that rich man. A lot of grown-ups do too. Some of them always want more than they have. They may have food for the day, clothing to wear, and a place to live. But they want more. They want lots of clothes. And they want bigger houses. These things cost money. So they work hard to get lots of money. And the more money they get, the more they want to have.

Some grown-ups become so busy trying to get money that they have no time to be with their family. And they have no time for God. Can their money keep them alive?— No, it can't. Can they use their money after they die?— No. This is because the dead are not able to do anything at all.—Ecclesiastes 9:5, 10.

Does this mean that it is wrong to have money?— No. We can buy food and clothing with money. The Bible says that it is a protection. (Ecclesiastes 7:12) But if we love money, then we are going to have trouble. We will be like that foolish rich man who stored up treasures for himself and was not rich toward God.

What does it mean to be rich toward God?— It means to put God first in our lives. Some people say that they believe in God. They think that believing is all that is needed. But are they really rich toward God?— No, they are like the rich man who forgot God.

Jesus never forgot his Father in heaven. He did not try to make a lot of money. And he did not own many material things. Jesus knew what was truly important in life. Do you know what that is?— It is being rich toward God.

Tell me, how can we be rich toward God?— We can be rich toward God by doing what pleases him. Jesus said: "I always do the things pleasing to him." (John 8:29) God likes it when we do the things he wants us to do. Now tell me, what things can you do to please God?— Yes, you can read the Bible, go to Christian meetings, pray to God, and help others learn about him. Those are truly the most important things in life.

Because Jesus was rich toward God, Jehovah took care of him. He gave Jesus the reward of living forever. If we are like Jesus, Jehovah will love us and take care of us too. So may we be like Jesus and never be like that rich man who forgot God.

Here are some Bible texts that show how to have the proper view of material things: Proverbs 23:4; 28:20; 1 Timothy 6:6-10; and Hebrews 13:5.

What is this child doing that is truly important?

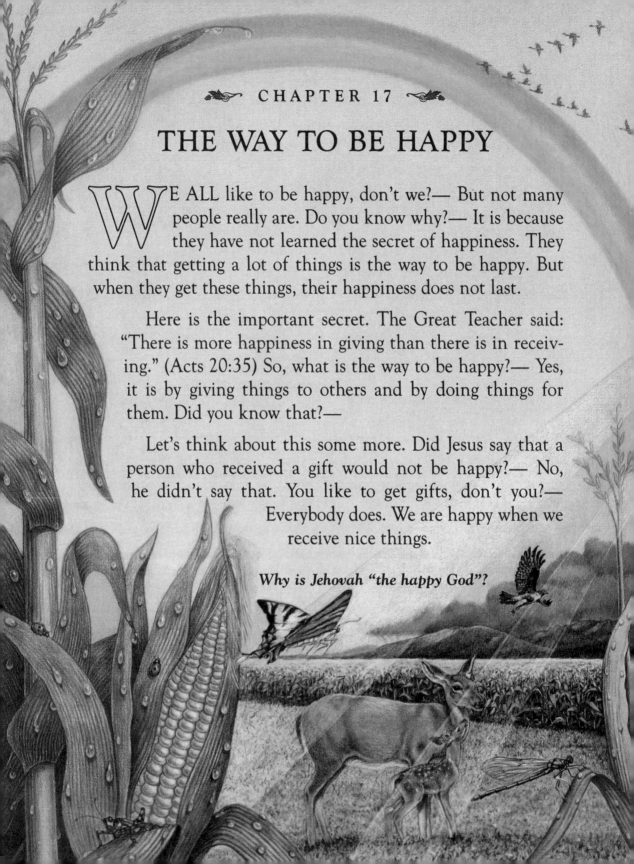

CHAPTER 17

THE WAY TO BE HAPPY

WE ALL like to be happy, don't we?— But not many people really are. Do you know why?— It is because they have not learned the secret of happiness. They think that getting a lot of things is the way to be happy. But when they get these things, their happiness does not last.

Here is the important secret. The Great Teacher said: "There is more happiness in giving than there is in receiving." (Acts 20:35) So, what is the way to be happy?— Yes, it is by giving things to others and by doing things for them. Did you know that?—

Let's think about this some more. Did Jesus say that a person who received a gift would not be happy?— No, he didn't say that. You like to get gifts, don't you?— Everybody does. We are happy when we receive nice things.

Why is Jehovah "the happy God"?

What can make you happier
than eating all of your cookies yourself?

But Jesus said that there is even more happiness when we give. So who would you say has given more things to people than anyone else?— Yes, Jehovah God.

The Bible says that God "gives to all persons life and breath and all things." He gives us rains from heaven and the sunshine too, so that plants grow and we have food to eat. (Acts 14: 17; 17:25) No wonder the Bible calls Jehovah "the happy God"! (1 Timothy 1:11) Giving to others is one of the things that make God happy. And when we give, it can make us happy too.

Now, what is there that we can give to other people? What would you say?— Sometimes a gift costs money. If it is a gift that you get at a store, you will have to pay for it. So if you want to give that kind of gift, you may have to save money until you have enough to buy the gift.

But not all gifts have to come from stores. For example, on a hot day, a glass of cold water really tastes good. So when you give that gift to a person who is thirsty, you can have the happiness that comes from giving.

Someday maybe you and your mother can bake cookies. That would be fun. But what could you do with some of those cookies that would make you even happier than eating all of them yourself?— Yes, you could make a gift of some of them to one of your friends. Would you like to do that sometime?—

What is Lydia
saying to
Paul and Luke?

Why is Lydia happy to provide
for Paul and Luke?

The Great Teacher and his apostles all knew the happiness of giving. Do you know what they gave to other people?— It was the best thing in the world! They knew the truth about God, and they gladly shared this good news with others. They did this without letting anyone give them money for what they gave.

One day the apostle Paul and his good friend the disciple Luke met a woman who also wanted to have the happiness of giving. They met her down by a river. Paul and Luke went there because they had heard that it was a place of prayer. And sure enough, when they arrived, they found some women praying.

Paul began to tell these women the good news about Jehovah God and his Kingdom. One of them was named Lydia, and she paid close attention. Afterward, Lydia wanted to do something to show that she really liked the good news that she had heard. So she urged Paul and Luke: "If you men have judged me to be faithful to Jehovah, enter into my house and stay." And she just made them come to her home.—Acts 16:13-15.

Lydia was glad to have these servants of God in her home. She loved them because they helped her to learn about Jehovah and Jesus and about how people could live forever. It made her happy to be able to give Paul and Luke food to eat and a place to rest. So Lydia's giving made her happy because she really wanted to give. That is something that we ought to remember. Someone may tell us that we have to give a gift. But if we really don't want to do it, the giving will not make us happy.

For example, what if you had some candy that you wanted to eat? If I told you that you had to give some of it to another child, would you be happy to give it away?— But what if you had some candy when you met a friend whom you liked very much? If you got the idea all by yourself to share some of it with your friend, wouldn't that make you happy?—

Sometimes we love a person so much that we want to give him everything and not keep back anything for ourselves. As we grow in our love for God, that is the way we should feel about Him.

The Great Teacher knew of a poor woman who felt that way. He saw her at the temple in Jerusalem. She had just two small coins; that is all she had. But she put both of them in the box as a contribution, or gift, for the temple. No one made her do it. Most of the people there did not even know what she had done. She did it because she wanted to and because she really loved Jehovah. It made her happy to be able to give. —Luke 21:1-4.

Why was this poor woman happy to give all she had?

There are many ways in which we can give. Can you think of some?— If we give because we really want to, we will be happy. That is why the Great Teacher tells us: "Practice giving." (Luke 6:38) If we do, we will be making other people happy. And we will be the happiest of all!

Let's read some more about how giving brings happiness, at Matthew 6:1-4; Luke 14:12-14; and 2 Corinthians 9:7.

96

CHAPTER 18

DO YOU REMEMBER TO SAY THANK YOU?

ID you eat a meal today?— Do you know who prepared it?— Perhaps your mother did or someone else, but why should we thank God for it?— Because God is the one who makes it possible for food to grow. However, we should also thank the one who prepared the meal or the one who served it to us.

Sometimes we forget to say thank you when others do kind things for us, don't we? When the Great Teacher was on earth, there were some lepers who forgot to say thank you.

Do you know what a leper is?— A leper is a person who has a sickness called leprosy. That sickness can even cause some of the person's flesh to fall off. When Jesus lived on earth, lepers had to live away from other people. And if a leper saw another person coming, he had to call out to warn that person to stay away from him. This was done so that other people would not get too close and maybe get the leper's sickness.

Jesus was very kind to lepers. One day on his way to Jerusalem, Jesus had to pass through a small town. When he got near the town, ten lepers came out to see him. They had heard that Jesus had power from God to cure all kinds of sicknesses.

The lepers did not come close to Jesus. They stood far off. But they believed that Jesus could take away their leprosy.

What is Jesus telling these lepers to do?

So when the lepers saw the Great Teacher, they called out to him: 'Jesus, Teacher, help us!'

Do you feel sorry for people who are sick?— Jesus did. He knew how sad it was to be a leper. So he answered them and said: "Go and show yourselves to the priests."—Luke 17:11-14.

Why did Jesus tell them to do this? It was because of the law that Jehovah had given to His people about lepers. This law said that God's priest was to look at the flesh of a leper. The priest would tell the leper when all of his sickness had left him. When he was well, he could live with well people again. —Leviticus 13:16, 17.

But these lepers still had their sickness. So did they go to the priest just as Jesus told them?— Yes, they did, right away. These men must have believed that Jesus would take away their sickness. What happened?

Well, while they were on their way to the priest, their sickness left them. Their flesh was healed. They were made well! Their belief in Jesus' power was rewarded. What joy they felt! But, now, what should they have done to show their thanks? What would you have done?—

One of the healed men came back to Jesus. He began giving glory to Jehovah, saying good things about God. That was the right thing to do because the power to heal him had come from God. The man also fell down at the feet of the Great Teacher and thanked him. He was so grateful for what Jesus had done.

What did this leper remember to do?

But what about the other nine men? Jesus asked: 'There were ten lepers who were made well, were there not? Where are the other nine? Did only one turn back to give glory to God?'

Yes, it is true. Only one of the ten gave glory, or praise, to God and came back to thank Jesus. And this person was a Samaritan, a man from another country. The other nine men did not thank God, and they did not thank Jesus.—Luke 17:15-19.

How can you imitate the leper who returned to Jesus?

Which of those men are you like? We want to be like the Samaritan man, don't we?— So when someone does something kind for us, what should we remember to do?— We ought to express our thanks. People often forget to say thank you. But it is good to say thank you. When we do, Jehovah God and his Son, Jesus, are pleased.

If you think about it, you will remember that people have done many things for you. For example, have you ever been sick?— You may never have been as sick as those ten lepers, but you may have had a bad cold or a pain in your stomach. Did someone take care of you?— They may have given you some medicine and done other things for you. Were you glad that they helped you to get better?—

The Samaritan man thanked Jesus for making him well, and this made Jesus happy. Do you think that your mother or father will be happy if you say thank you when they do things for you?— Yes, they will.

Some people do things for you every day or every week.

It may be their job to do these things. They may even be happy to do them. But you may forget to say thank you. Your school-teacher may work hard to help you learn. This is her work. But she will be pleased if you thank her for helping you to learn.

Sometimes people just do little things for you. Does anyone ever hold a door open for you? Or does anyone ever pass food to you at the dinner table? It is good to say thank you for even these little things.

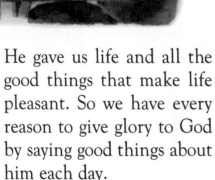

If we remember to say thank you to people on earth, then we are more likely to remember to say thank you to our Father in heaven. And how many things there are for which to thank Jehovah!

Why is it important to remember to say thank you?

He gave us life and all the good things that make life pleasant. So we have every reason to give glory to God by saying good things about him each day.

Regarding the expressing of thanks, read Psalm 92:1 (91:1, "Dy"); Ephesians 5:20; Colossians 3:17; and 1 Thessalonians 5:18.

CHAPTER 19

IS IT RIGHT TO FIGHT?

DO YOU know any boys or girls who try to act big and tough?— Do you like to be with them? Or would you rather be with someone who is kind and wants peace?— The Great Teacher said: "Happy are the peaceable, since they will be called 'sons of God.'"—Matthew 5:9.

But sometimes other people do things that make us angry. Isn't that true?— So we may feel like getting even with them. Once this happened to Jesus' disciples when they were traveling with Jesus toward Jerusalem. Let me tell you about it.

When they had gone some distance, Jesus sent a few of his disciples ahead to a Samaritan village to find a place for them to rest. But the people there did not want them to stay, since the Samaritans had a different religion. And they didn't like anyone that went to the city of Jerusalem to worship.

What did James and John want to do to get even with the Samaritans?

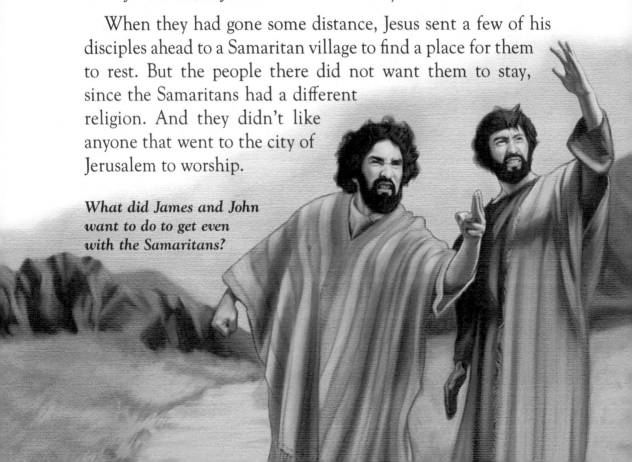

If that had happened to you, what would you have done? Would you have got angry? Would you have wanted to get even with them?— That is what the disciples James and John wanted to do. They said to Jesus: 'Do you want us to tell fire to come down from heaven and destroy them?' No wonder Jesus called them Sons of Thunder! But Jesus told them it was not right to treat other people that way.—Luke 9:51-56; Mark 3:17.

It is true that people may be mean to us at times. Other children may not want us to play in their games. They may even say: "We don't want you around here." When something like that happens, it can make us feel bad, can't it? We may feel like doing something to get even with them. But should we?—

Why not get your Bible? Let's turn to Proverbs chapter 24, verse 29. There it reads: "Do not say: 'Just as he did to me, so I am going to do to him. I shall repay to each one according to his acting.'"

What does that mean to you?— It is saying that we should not try to get even. We should not be mean to a person just because he was mean to us. But what if someone tries to pick a fight with you? He may try to get you angry by calling you names. He may laugh at you and say that you're scared. Suppose he calls you a coward. What should you do? Should you let yourself get into a fight?—

Again, let's see what the Bible says. Turn to Matthew chapter 5, verse 39. There Jesus says: "Do not resist him that is wicked; but whoever slaps you on your right cheek, turn the other also to him." What do you think Jesus meant by that? Did he mean that if someone hits you with his fist on one side of your face, you should let him hit you on the other side?—

No, Jesus did not mean that at all. A slap is not like a hit with the fist. It is more like a push or a shove. A person may slap us to pick a fight. He wants us to get angry. And if we get angry and we push or shove back, what happens?— We will probably get into a fight.

But Jesus did not want his followers to get into fights. So he said that if someone slaps us, we should not slap him back. We should not become angry and get into a fight. If we do, we show that we are no better than the one who started the fight.

What should we do if someone tries to pick a fight with us?

If trouble starts, what do you think is the best thing to do?— It is to walk away. The other person may push or shove you a few more times. But that will probably be the end of it. When you walk away, it does not mean that you are weak. It means that you are strong for what is right.

But what if you let yourself get into a fight and you win? What could happen then?— The one you beat up could come back with some friends. They might even hurt you with a big stick or a knife. So, can you see now why Jesus did not want us to get into fights?—

What should we do if we see other people fighting? Should we take sides with one or the other?— The Bible tells us what is right. Turn to Proverbs chapter 26, verse 17. It says: "As one grabbing hold of the ears of a dog is anyone passing by that is becoming furious at the quarrel that is not his."

What would happen if you grabbed hold of the ears of a dog? It would hurt the dog, and he would snap at you, wouldn't he? The more the dog tried to get loose, the harder you would have to hold on to the ears and the more excited the dog would get. If you let him go, he would probably bite you hard. But can you just stand there and hold his ears forever?—

Well, that is the kind of trouble that we would be in if we got mixed up in a fight between other people. We may not know who started the fight or why they are fighting. One person may be getting beaten up,

*How is getting mixed up in other people's fights
like grabbing hold of the ears of a dog?
You may get hurt, so don't do it!*

105

but perhaps he stole something from the other one. If we helped him, we would be helping a thief. That would not be good, would it?

So, what should you do if you see a fight?— If it is at school, you can run and tell a teacher. And if it is away from school, you can call one of your parents or a policeman. Yes, even when other people want to fight, we should be peaceable.

True disciples of Jesus do all they can to avoid getting into fights. In this way we show that we are strong for what is right. The Bible says that a disciple of Jesus "does not need to fight, but needs to be gentle toward all."—2 Timothy 2:24.

Now let's look at more good counsel that will help us stay out of fights: Romans 12:17-21 and 1 Peter 3:10, 11.

What should you do if you see a fight?

CHAPTER 20

DO YOU ALWAYS
WANT TO BE FIRST?

DO YOU know anyone who always wants to be first?—
He may push someone away so that he can be first in
line. Have you seen that happen?— The Great Teacher
saw even grown-ups try to get the first, or most important,
places. And he did not like it. Let's see what happened.

The Bible tells us that Jesus was invited to a big meal at the
home of a Pharisee, who was an important religious leader.
After Jesus arrived, he began to watch other guests come in and
choose the best places. So he told a story to those who had been
invited. Would you like to hear it?—

Have you seen people try to be first?

Jesus said: 'When someone invites you to a wedding feast, do not pick the best, or most important, place.' Do you know why Jesus said that?— He explained that someone more important may have been invited. So, as you can see in the picture, the one giving the feast comes and says: 'Let this man have the place, and you go over there.' How would the guest feel then?— He would feel shame because all the other guests would watch him move to the less important place.

Jesus was showing that it is not right to want the highest place. So he said: 'When you are invited to a wedding feast, go and sit in the lowest place. Then the one who has invited you may come and say, "Friend, go on up higher." You will then have honor in front of all the other guests as you move to the better place.'—Luke 14:1, 7-11.

Did you get the point of Jesus' story?— Let's give an example to see if you did. Imagine that you are getting on a crowded bus. Should you hurry to get a seat and let an older person stand?— Would Jesus like it if you did that?—

Someone may say that it does not make any difference to Jesus what we do. But do you believe that?— When Jesus was at that big meal at the home of the Pharisee, he watched the people as they chose their seats. Don't you think that he is just as interested in what we do today?— Now that Jesus is in heaven, he certainly is in a good position to watch us.

When someone tries to be first, it can cause trouble. Often there is an argument, and people get angry. Sometimes this happens when children go for a bus ride together. As soon as the bus doors are opened, the children rush to be first. They want the best seats, the ones near the windows. What may happen then?— Yes, they may get mad at one another.

Wanting to be first can cause a lot of trouble. It even caused trouble among Jesus' apostles. As we learned in Chapter 6 of this book, they argued among themselves about who was the greatest. What did Jesus do then?— Yes, he corrected them. But later they had another argument. Let's see how it started.

The apostles, along with others, are traveling with Jesus for the last time to the city of Jerusalem.

What lesson was Jesus teaching when he told about those taking the best, or first, seats?

Jesus has been talking to them about his Kingdom, so James and John have been thinking about ruling as kings with him. They have even spoken with their mother, Salome, about it. (Matthew 27:56; Mark 15:40) So when they are on their way to Jerusalem, Salome comes to Jesus, bows before him, and asks a favor.

"What do you want?" Jesus asks. She answers that she would like Jesus to let her sons sit right next to him in his Kingdom, one at his right hand and the other at his left. Well, when the ten other apostles learn what James and John have had their mother ask for, how do you think they feel?—

Yes, they are very angry at James and John. So Jesus gives all his apostles some good advice. Jesus tells them that the rulers of

What does Salome ask Jesus for, and what is the result?

the nations love to be big and important. They want to have a high position where everyone obeys them. But Jesus tells his followers that they should not be that way. Rather, Jesus says: "Whoever wants to be first among you must be your slave." Think of that!—Matthew 20:20-28.

Do you know what a slave does?— He serves other people, not expecting others to serve him. He takes the lowest place, not the first place. He acts as the least important one, not the most important. And remember, Jesus said that the one who wants to be first should act like a slave toward others.

Now, what do you think that means for us?— Would a slave argue with his master over who is going to get the best seat? Or would he argue about who is going to eat first? What do you think?— Jesus explained that a slave always puts his master before himself.—Luke 17:7-10.

So rather than trying to be first, what should we do?— Yes, we should be like a slave to others. And that means putting others ahead of ourselves. It means considering that others are more important than we are. Can you think of ways that you can put others first?— Why not go back to pages 40 and 41 and look again at some of the ways that you can put others first by serving them.

You will remember that the Great Teacher put others ahead of himself by serving them. The last evening he spent with his apostles, he even got down and washed their feet. If we also put others first by serving them, we will be pleasing both the Great Teacher and his Father, Jehovah God.

Let's read some more Bible texts that encourage us to put others ahead of ourselves: Luke 9:48; Romans 12:3; and Philippians 2:3, 4.

CHAPTER 21

SHOULD WE BRAG ABOUT ANYTHING?

WHAT does it mean to brag? Do you know?— Here is an example. Have you ever tried to do something that you are not very good at? Maybe you tried to kick a soccer ball. Or maybe you tried to skip rope. Did anyone ever say, "Ha! Ha! Ha! I can do that better than you can"?— Well, that person was bragging.

How do you feel when others do that? Do you like it?— Then, how do you think others feel if you brag about yourself?— Is it kind to tell someone else, "I'm better than you"?— Does Jehovah like people who do that?—

The Great Teacher knew people who thought they were better than others. They would brag, or boast, about themselves and look down on everyone else. So one day Jesus told them a story to show them how wrong it was to brag about themselves. Let's listen to it.

The story is about a Pharisee and a tax collector. Now, the Pharisees were religious teachers, who often acted as if they were more righteous or holier than other people. The Pharisee in Jesus' story went up to God's temple in Jerusalem to pray.

Jesus said that a tax collector also went up to the temple to pray. Most people did not like tax collectors. They felt that the tax collectors were trying to cheat them. And it is true that many tax collectors were not always honest.

At the temple, the Pharisee began praying to God this way: 'O God, I thank you that I am not a sinner like other people. I do not cheat people or do other bad things. I am not like that tax collector over there. I am a righteous man. I go without food twice a week so that I have more time to think about you. And I give to the temple a tenth of all the things that I get.' The Pharisee really thought that he was better than others, didn't he?— And he told God about it too.

But the tax collector was not like that. He would not even raise his eyes toward heaven when he prayed. He kept standing at a distance with his head bowed. The tax collector was very sorry about his sins, and he beat his chest in grief. He did not try to tell God how good he was. Rather, he prayed: 'O God, be kind to me a sinner.'

Which of these two men do you think was pleasing to God? Was it the Pharisee, the one who thought he was so good? Or was it the tax collector, the one who felt sorry about his sins?—

Why was God pleased with the tax collector but not the Pharisee?

Jesus said that the tax collector was the one pleasing to God. Why? Jesus explained: 'Because everyone who tries to make it look as if he is better than other people will be brought low. But he that is lowly in his own eyes will be raised up.'—Luke 18:9-14.

What was the lesson that Jesus was teaching in his story?—He was teaching that it is wrong to think that we are better than others. We may not say that we think we are, but by the way we act, we could show that we think we are. Have you ever acted that way?— Consider the apostle Peter.

When Jesus told his apostles that they would all leave him when he was arrested, Peter bragged: '*Even if everyone else leaves you, I never will!*' But Peter was wrong. He was too sure of himself. He did leave Jesus. However, he returned, as we will learn in Chapter 30 of this book.—Matthew 26:31-33.

Let's take a modern-day example. Perhaps you and a classmate are being asked some questions at school. What if you are able to give the answers right away, but the other student is not able to? Of course, you feel good when you know the answers. But would it be kind to compare yourself with the one who is slow to answer?— Is it right to try to make yourself look good by making the other person look bad?—

That is what the Pharisee did. He bragged that he was better than the tax collector. But the Great Teacher said that the Pharisee was wrong. It is true that one person may be able to do a certain thing better than someone else can. But that does not mean that he is really a better person.

So if we know more than another person, is that a good reason to brag?— Think about it. Did we make our own brain?— No, God is the one who gave each of us a brain. And most of the things we know, we learned from someone else. Maybe we read things in a book. Or perhaps someone told us about them. Even if we figure something out by ourselves, how did we do it?— Yes, by using the brain that God gave us.

Does it make you a better person if you know more than someone else?

When a person tries hard, the kind thing is for you to say something that makes him feel good. Tell him that you like what he did. Maybe you can even help him to do better. That is what you would like people to do for you, isn't it?—

Some people are stronger than others. What if you are stronger than your brother or sister? Is that any reason for you to brag?— No, it isn't. It is the food we eat that helps us to grow strong. And God gives the sunshine and the rain and everything else that is needed to make food grow, doesn't he?— So, then, it is God we should thank if we grow strong.—Acts 14: 16, 17.

Why is it wrong to brag if we are stronger than another person?

None of us like to hear someone brag about himself, do we?— Let's remember Jesus' words: 'Just as you want other people to do to you, do the same way to them.' If we do that, we will never be like the Pharisee who bragged about himself in the story that the Great Teacher told. —Luke 6:31.

115

Once someone called Jesus good. Did the Great Teacher say, 'Yes, I am good'?— No, he didn't. Instead, he said: "Nobody is good, except one, God." (Mark 10:18) Even though the Great Teacher was perfect, he did not brag about himself. Rather, he gave all praise to his Father, Jehovah.

So, is there anyone whom we can brag about?— Yes, there is. We can brag about our Creator, Jehovah God. When we see a beautiful sunset or some other marvel of creation, we can tell someone, 'Our wonderful God, Jehovah, made this!' Let's always be ready to speak about the grand things Jehovah has already done and will do in the future.

Read what the Scriptures say about bragging, or boasting, and learn how we should avoid bragging about ourselves: Proverbs 16:5, 18; Jeremiah 9:23, 24; 1 Corinthians 4:7; and 13:4.

What is this boy bragging about?

CHAPTER 22

WHY WE SHOULD NOT LIE

SUPPOSE that a girl tells her mother: "Yes, I will come home right after school." But then she stays and plays with her friends and later tells her mother: "My teacher made me stay after school." Would it be all right to say something like that?—

Or perhaps a boy tells his father: "No, I didn't kick the ball in the house." But what if he really did? Would it be wrong to say that he didn't?—

The Great Teacher showed us the right thing to do. He said: 'Just let your word *Yes* mean Yes, and your *No*, No; for anything else is from the wicked one.' (Matthew 5:37) What did Jesus mean by that?— He meant that we should do what we say.

There is a story in the Bible that shows how important it is to tell the truth. It is about two people who said that they were disciples of Jesus. Let's see what happened.

What has this boy done wrong?

117

Less than two months after Jesus dies, many people from faraway places come to Jerusalem for an important festival of the Jews called Pentecost. The apostle Peter gives a wonderful talk in which he tells the people about Jesus, whom Jehovah raised from the dead. This is the first time many of those who have come to Jerusalem learn about Jesus. Now they want to know more. So, what do they do?

They stay longer than they expected. But after a while, some of them run out of money, and they need help so that they can buy food. The disciples in Jerusalem want to help the visitors out. So, many of them sell things that they own and bring the money to Jesus' apostles. Then the apostles give the money to the ones who need it.

What lie is Ananias telling Peter?

Ananias and his wife, Sapphira, who are members of the Christian congregation in Jerusalem, sell a field they own. No one tells them to sell it. They decide that for themselves. But what they do is not because they love the new disciples of Jesus. Actually, Ananias and Sapphira want to make people think that they are better than they really are. So they decide to say that they are giving all the money to help others. They are really going to give only a part of it but say that they are giving it all. What do you think of that?—

Well, Ananias comes to see the apostles. He gives the money to them. God, of course, knows that he is not giving it all. So God lets the apostle Peter know that Ananias is not being truthful about the matter.

Then Peter says: 'Ananias, why have you let Satan cause you to do this? The field was yours. You didn't have to sell it. And even after you sold the field, it was up to you to decide what you would do with the money. But why are you pretending to give all the money when you are giving only part of it? By this you are lying, not just to us, but to God.'

It is that serious. Ananias is lying! He isn't doing what he says he is doing. He is only pretending to do it. The Bible tells us what happens next. It says: 'On hearing Peter's words, Ananias falls down and dies.' God strikes Ananias dead! Afterward, his body is carried outside and buried.

What happens to Ananias because he lied?

About three hours later, Sapphira comes in. She does not know what happened to her husband. So Peter asks her: 'Did you two sell the field for the amount of money that you gave us?'

Sapphira answers: 'Yes, we sold the field for just that amount.' But that is a lie! They kept for themselves some of the money from the sale of the field. So God strikes Sapphira dead too.—Acts 5:1-11.

What should we learn from what happened to Ananias and Sapphira?— It teaches us that God does not like liars. He always wants us to tell the truth. But many people say that it is all right to tell lies. Do you think that those people are correct?— Did you know that all the sickness, pain, and death on the earth came about because of a lie?—

Remember, the Devil lied to the first woman, Eve. He told her that she would not die if she disobeyed God and ate the fruit that God had said she should not eat. Eve believed the Devil and ate the fruit. She got Adam to eat it too. Now they were sinners, and all their children would be born sinners. And because they were sinners, all of Adam's children suffered and died. How did all the trouble start?— It started with a lie.

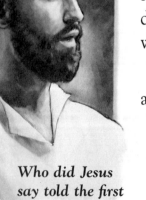

No wonder Jesus said that the Devil "is a liar and the father of the lie"! He was the first one who told a lie. When anyone tells a lie, he is doing what the Devil did first. We should think about this if we ever feel tempted to tell a lie.—John 8:44.

Who did Jesus say told the first lie, and what was the result?

120

When is it that you may feel tempted to lie?— Isn't it when you have done something wrong?— Even though you do not mean to, you may break something. If you're asked about it, should you say that your brother or sister did it? Or should you pretend that you don't know how it happened?—

What if you were supposed to do your homework but you did only part of it? Should you say that you did it all, even if you did not?— We should remember Ananias and Sapphira. They did not tell the whole truth. And God showed how bad that was by striking them dead.

So no matter what we may do, it will always make matters worse if we lie about it, and we shouldn't even tell only half of the truth. The Bible says: "Speak truth." It also says: "Do not be lying to one another." Jehovah always speaks the truth, and he expects us to do the same.—Ephesians 4:25; Colossians 3:9.

We should always tell the truth. That is the point made at Exodus 20:16; Proverbs 6:16-19; 12:19; 14:5; 16:6; and Hebrews 4:13.

When may you be tempted to lie?

CHAPTER 23

THE REASON
PEOPLE GET SICK

DO YOU know anyone who is sick?— You probably get sick sometimes yourself. You may get a cold, or your stomach may ache. Some people are very sick. They cannot even stand up without someone to help them. This often happens when people get very old.

Everyone gets sick sometimes. Do you know why people get sick, grow old, and die?— One day a man who could not walk was brought to Jesus, and Jesus showed why people get sick and die. Let me tell you about it.

Jesus was staying at a house in a town near the Sea of Galilee. A crowd of people came to see him. So many people came that there was no room for others to enter the house. No one could even get near the door. Still, people kept coming! One group of people brought a paralyzed man who could not even walk. It took four men to carry him on a little bed, or cot.

Do you know why they wanted to bring this sick man to Jesus?— They had faith that Jesus could help him. They believed that Jesus could heal him from that sickness. Do you know how they got that paralyzed man to Jesus with all those people in the house?—

Well, the picture you see here shows how they did it. First, they carried the man up onto the roof. It was a flat roof. Then, they made a big hole in it. Finally, they lowered the sick man on his cot right through that hole and into the room below. What faith they had!

All the people in the house were surprised when they saw what was happening. The paralyzed man on the cot came right down into their midst. Was Jesus angry when he saw what the men had done?— Not at all! He was glad to see that they had faith. He said to the paralyzed man: *"Your sins are forgiven."*

Some of the people did not think it was right for Jesus to say that. They did not think that he could forgive sins. So to show that he really could, Jesus said to the man: "Get up, pick up your cot, and go to your home."

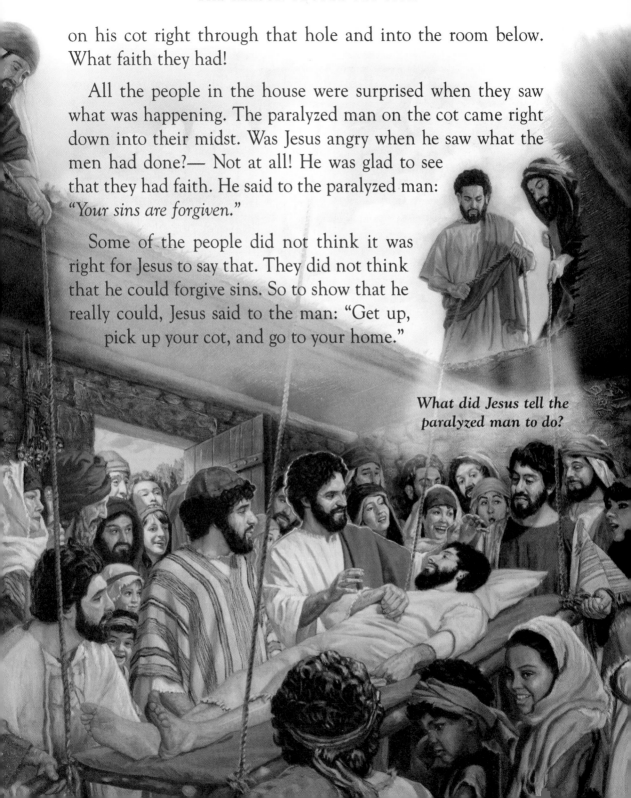

What did Jesus tell the paralyzed man to do?

When Jesus said that, the man was healed! He was not paralyzed anymore. Now he was able to get up all by himself and walk. The people who saw this miracle were amazed. Never in all their lives had they seen anything as wonderful as that! They praised Jehovah for giving them this Great Teacher, who could even heal people of their sicknesses.—Mark 2:1-12.

What do we learn from this miracle?— We learn that Jesus has the power to forgive sins and to make sick people well. But we also learn something else, something very important. *We learn that people get sick because of sin.*

What do we learn from this miracle?

Since we all get sick sometimes, does this mean that we are all sinners?— Yes, the Bible says that all of us are born with sin. Do you know what it means to be born with sin?— It means that we are born imperfect. We sometimes do things wrong, even though we don't want to. Do you know how we all came to have sin?—

We got this way because the first man, Adam, did not obey God. He sinned when he broke God's law. And we all got sin from Adam. Do you know how we got our sin from him? Let me try to explain it in a way that you can understand.

Maybe you have helped someone bake bread in a pan. What will happen to the bread if there is a dent in the pan?

Do you know?— That same mark, or dent, will show on all the bread you make in that pan, won't it?—

Adam was like that pan, and we are like the bread. He became imperfect when he broke God's law. It was as though he had received a dent, or a bad mark. So when he had children, what would they be like?— All his children would receive this same mark of imperfection.

How did all of us come to have sin?

Most children are not born with some big imperfection that you can see. They do not have an arm or a leg missing. But the imperfection they have is serious enough that they become sick and, in time, die.

Of course, some people get sick more often than others. Why is that? Is it because they are born with more sin?— No, everybody is born with the same amount of sin. We are all born imperfect. So, sooner or later, everybody will have some kind of sickness. Even people who try to obey all of God's laws and who do nothing really bad can get sick.

Then, why do some people get sick more often than others?— There are many reasons. It may be that they do not have enough food to eat. Or they may not eat the right kind of food. They may eat too much cake and candy. Another reason may be that they stay up too late at night and do not get enough sleep. Or they may not dress warmly enough before they go out into the cold. Some people's bodies are too weak, and they can't

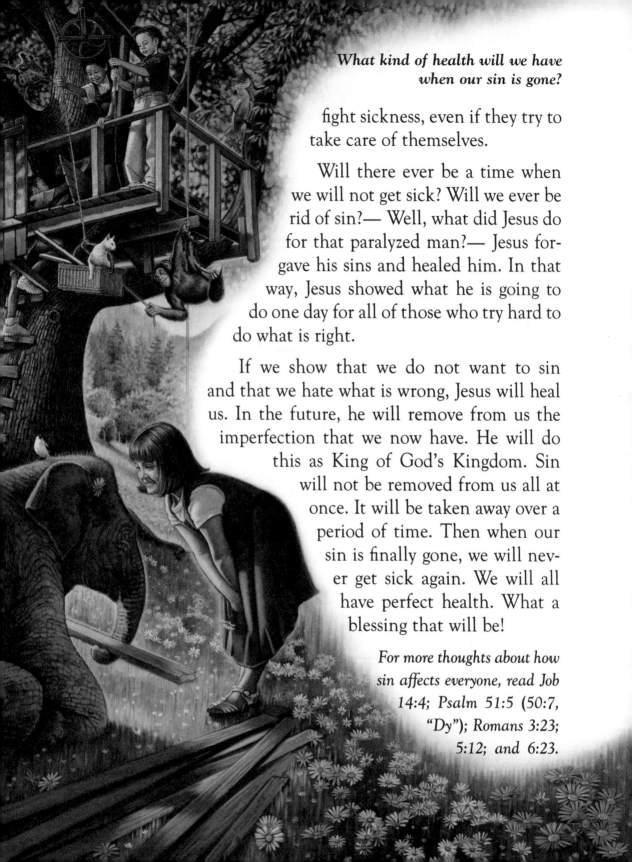

What kind of health will we have when our sin is gone?

fight sickness, even if they try to take care of themselves.

Will there ever be a time when we will not get sick? Will we ever be rid of sin?— Well, what did Jesus do for that paralyzed man?— Jesus forgave his sins and healed him. In that way, Jesus showed what he is going to do one day for all of those who try hard to do what is right.

If we show that we do not want to sin and that we hate what is wrong, Jesus will heal us. In the future, he will remove from us the imperfection that we now have. He will do this as King of God's Kingdom. Sin will not be removed from us all at once. It will be taken away over a period of time. Then when our sin is finally gone, we will never get sick again. We will all have perfect health. What a blessing that will be!

For more thoughts about how sin affects everyone, read Job 14:4; Psalm 51:5 (50:7, "Dy"); Romans 3:23; 5:12; and 6:23.

CHAPTER 24

NEVER BECOME A THIEF!

HAS anyone ever stolen something from you?— How did that make you feel?— Whoever stole it was a thief, and nobody likes a thief. How do you think a person becomes a thief? Is he born that way?—

We just learned that people are born with sin. So all of us are imperfect. But nobody is born a thief. A thief may come from a good family. His parents, his brothers, and his sisters may be honest. But a person's own desire for such things as money and what money can buy may cause him to become a thief.

Who would you say was the first thief?— Let's think about it. The Great Teacher knew that person when he was in heaven. That thief was an angel. But since God had made all angels perfect, how did that angel become a thief?— Well, as we learned in Chapter 8 of this book, he wanted something that was not his. Do you remember what it was?—

After God created the first man and woman, that angel wanted them to worship him. He had no right to their worship. Their worship belonged to God. But he stole it! By getting Adam and Eve to worship him, the angel became a thief. He became Satan the Devil.

What is it that causes a person to become a thief?— *A desire for what does not belong to him.* This desire can become so strong that it can make even good people do bad things. Sometimes, those people who become thieves never do turn around and do what is good again. One of them was an apostle of Jesus. His name was Judas Iscariot.

Judas knew that it was wrong to steal because he had been taught God's Law from the time he was a little boy. He knew that God had once even spoken from heaven and told his people: "You must not steal." (Exodus 20:15) When Judas grew up, he met the Great Teacher and became one of his disciples. Later, Jesus even picked Judas to be one of his 12 apostles.

Jesus and his apostles traveled together. They ate their meals together. And all the money the group had was kept in a box. Jesus gave that box to Judas to take care of. Of course, the money did not belong to Judas. But do you know what Judas did after a while?—

Judas started to take money from the box when he wasn't supposed to. He would take it when the others were not looking, and he even tried to find ways to get more of it. He began to think about money all the time. Let's see what this wrong desire led to just a few days before the Great Teacher was killed.

Mary, a sister of Jesus' friend Lazarus, took some very fine oil and poured it on the feet of Jesus. But Judas complained. Do you know why?— He said that it was because the oil should have been sold and the money given to poor people. But he really wanted to get more money in the box so that he could steal it.—John 12:1-6.

Jesus told Judas not to make trouble for Mary, who had been so kind. Judas did not like it when Jesus told him that, so he went to the chief priests, who were enemies of Jesus. They wanted to arrest Jesus, but they wanted to do it at night so that people could not see them.

Judas told the priests: 'I will tell you how you can get Jesus if you give me money. How much will you give me?'

'We will give you thirty pieces of silver,' the priests answered.—Matthew 26:14-16.

Judas took the money. It was just as if he was selling the Great Teacher to those men! Can you imagine anyone doing such a bad thing?— Well, that is the kind of thing that happens when a person becomes a thief and steals money. He loves money more than he loves other people or even God.

Maybe you will say, 'I will never love anything more than I love Jehovah God.' It is good that you feel that way. When Jesus chose Judas as an apostle, that is probably how Judas felt. Others who became thieves may have felt that way too. Let's talk about some of them.

One was a servant of God named Achan, who lived long before the Great Teacher was born. Achan saw a

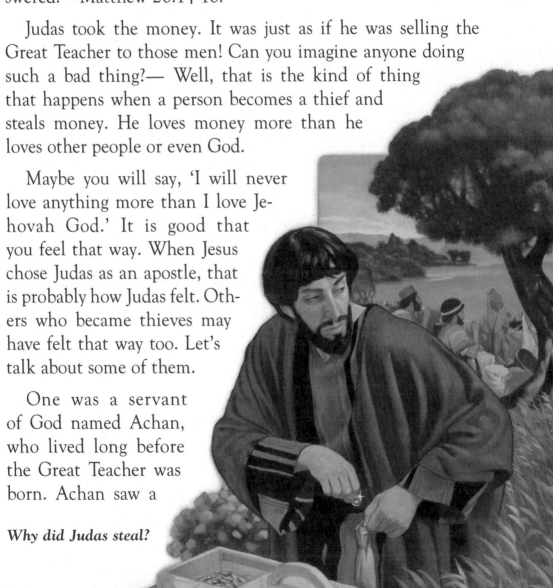

Why did Judas steal?

**What bad things
are Achan and David
thinking about?**

beautiful robe, a bar of gold,
and some pieces of silver.
They did not belong to him.
The Bible says they belonged
to Jehovah because they had
been taken from enemies
of God's people. But Achan
wanted them so much that
he stole them.—Josh-
ua 6:19; 7:11, 20-22.

Here is another ex-
ample. Long ago, Je-
hovah chose David to
be king over the peo-
ple of Israel. One day,
David began to look
at the beautiful wom-
an Bath-sheba. He kept
looking at Bath-sheba
and thinking about tak-
ing her home to be with
him. However, she was
Uriah's wife. What should David have
done?—

David should have stopped thinking
about having Bath-sheba. But he didn't.

In what way was Absalom a thief?

So David took her home. And then he had Uriah killed. Why did David do these bad things?— Because he kept wanting a woman who belonged to someone else.—2 Samuel 11:2-27.

Because David was sorry, Jehovah let him live. But now David had a lot of trouble. His son Absalom wanted to take David's place as king. So when people came to see David, Absalom would put his arms around them and kiss them. The Bible says: "Absalom kept *stealing* the hearts of the men of Israel." He got those people to want him to be king instead of David.—2 Samuel 15:1-12.

Have you ever wanted something very much, as Achan, David, and Absalom did?— If that thing belongs to someone else, to take it without permission is stealing. Do you remember what the first thief, Satan, wanted?— He wanted people to worship him rather than God. So Satan was stealing when he got Adam and Eve to obey him.

When a person owns something, he has the right to say who may use it. For example, you may go to play with other children in their house. Would it be all right to take something from there and bring it to your house?— Not unless the father or mother tells you that you can. If you take something home without asking them, that is stealing.

Why might you be tempted to steal?— Because you want something that does not belong to you. Even if another person doesn't see you take it, who does?— Jehovah God. And we need to remember that God hates stealing. So love for God and your neighbor will help you never to become a thief.

The Bible makes clear that it is wrong to steal. Please read Mark 10:17-19; Romans 13:9; and Ephesians 4:28.

CHAPTER 25

CAN THOSE WHO DO BAD THINGS CHANGE?

WOULDN'T it be wonderful if everyone did what was good?— But nobody always does good things. Do you know why we all do bad things sometimes, even when we want to do what is good?— Because all of us are born with sin. But some people do many very bad things. They hate other people and hurt them on purpose. Do you think that they can change and learn to be good?—

Look at the young man guarding the outer garments of those who are throwing stones at Stephen. His Hebrew name is Saul, but his Roman name is Paul. He is glad that Stephen, who is a disciple of the Great Teacher, is being killed. Let's see why Saul does such bad things.

Saul belongs to a Jewish religious group called the Pharisees. The Pharisees have God's Word, but they pay more attention to the teachings of some of their own religious leaders. This makes Saul do bad things.

When Stephen is arrested in Jerusalem, Saul is right there. Stephen is taken to court, where some of the judges are Pharisees. Even though bad things are said about Stephen, he is not afraid. He speaks right up and gives the judges a good witness about Jehovah God and about Jesus.

But those judges do not like what they hear. They already know a lot about Jesus. In fact, only a short time before this, they had Jesus put to death! But afterward, Jehovah took Jesus back to heaven. Now, instead of changing their ways, the judges fight against the disciples of Jesus.

The judges grab hold of Stephen and take him outside the city. They knock him down and throw stones at him. And, as you can see in the picture, Saul is there watching. He thinks it is right to kill Stephen.

Do you know why Saul thought that way?— Well, all his life Saul had been a Pharisee, and he believed that the teachings of the Pharisees were right. He looked to those men as an example, so he copied them.—Acts 7:54-60.

After Stephen is killed, what does Saul do?— Why, he tries to get rid of the rest of Jesus' disciples! He goes right into their homes and drags out both men and women. Then he has them thrown into prison. Many of the disciples have to leave Jerusalem, but they do not stop preaching about Jesus.—Acts 8:1-4.

Why does Saul think that it is right to kill Stephen?

This causes Saul to hate Jesus' disciples even more. So he goes to High Priest Caiaphas and gets approval to arrest Christians in the city of Damascus. Saul wants to bring them as prisoners to Jerusalem to have them punished. But when he is on the way to Damascus, an amazing thing happens.

A light flashes from heaven, and a voice says: "Saul, Saul, why are you persecuting me?" It is Jesus speaking from heaven! The light is so bright that it makes Saul blind, and the people with Saul have to lead him to Damascus.

Three days later Jesus appears in a vision to one of his disciples in Damascus named Ananias. Jesus tells Ananias to visit Saul, to take away his blindness, and to talk to him. When Ananias speaks to him, Saul accepts the truth about Jesus. He gets his eyesight back. His entire way of life changes, and he becomes a faithful servant of God.—Acts 9:1-22.

Do you see now why Saul used to do bad things?— It was because he had been taught wrong things. He followed men who were not faithful to God. And he belonged to a group of people who put the ideas of men ahead of the Word of God. But why does Saul change his life and begin to do good, even though other Pharisees continue to fight against God?— It is because Saul does not really hate the truth. So when he is shown what is right, he is ready to do it.

Do you know who Saul later became?— Yes, he became known as the apostle Paul, an apostle of Jesus. And remember, Paul wrote more books of the Bible than any other person.

There are many people like Saul who can change. But it is not easy because there is someone working very hard to make

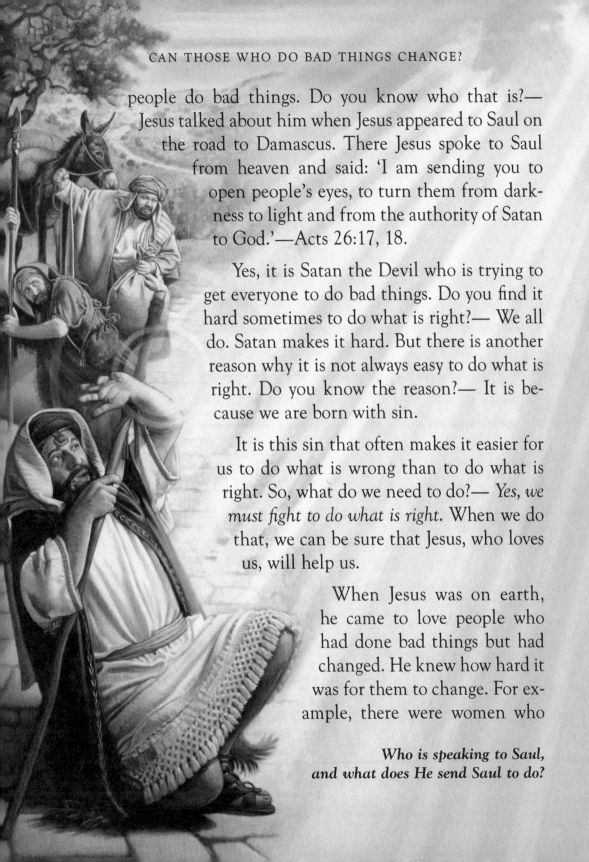

people do bad things. Do you know who that is?—
Jesus talked about him when Jesus appeared to Saul on
the road to Damascus. There Jesus spoke to Saul
from heaven and said: 'I am sending you to
open people's eyes, to turn them from darkness to light and from the authority of Satan
to God.'—Acts 26:17, 18.

Yes, it is Satan the Devil who is trying to
get everyone to do bad things. Do you find it
hard sometimes to do what is right?— We all
do. Satan makes it hard. But there is another
reason why it is not always easy to do what is
right. Do you know the reason?— It is because we are born with sin.

It is this sin that often makes it easier for
us to do what is wrong than to do what is
right. So, what do we need to do?— *Yes, we
must fight to do what is right.* When we do
that, we can be sure that Jesus, who loves
us, will help us.

When Jesus was on earth,
he came to love people who
had done bad things but had
changed. He knew how hard it
was for them to change. For example, there were women who

*Who is speaking to Saul,
and what does He send Saul to do?*

had sex relations with many men. This, of course, was bad. The Bible calls these women harlots, or prostitutes.

Once, a woman like that heard about Jesus, and she came to where he was at the house of a Pharisee. She poured oil on Jesus' feet and wiped off her tears from his feet with her hair. She was very sorry for her sins, so Jesus forgave her. But the Pharisee did not think she should be forgiven.—Luke 7:36-50.

Do you know what Jesus said to some of the Pharisees?— He told them: "The harlots are going ahead of you into the kingdom of God." (Matthew 21:31) Jesus said this because the harlots believed him, and they changed their bad ways. But the Pharisees kept doing bad things to Jesus' disciples.

So when the Bible shows that what we are doing is bad, we should be willing to change. And when we learn what Jehovah wants us to do, we should be eager to do it. Then Jehovah will be happy with us and will give us everlasting life.

To help us avoid doing what is bad, let's read together Psalm 119:9-11 (118:9-11, "Dy"); Proverbs 3:5-7; and 12:15.

Why did Jesus forgive this woman who had done bad things?

WHY IT IS HARD TO DO GOOD

WHEN Saul did bad things, who was pleased?— Satan the Devil was. But the religious leaders of the Jews were too. Then when Saul became a disciple of the Great Teacher and was called Paul, those religious leaders began to hate him. So, can you see why it is hard for a disciple of Jesus to do good?—

The high priest who was named Ananias once told men to hit Paul in the face. Ananias even tried to have Paul put in prison. Paul suffered a lot when he became a disciple of Jesus. For example, bad people beat Paul and tried to kill him with big stones.—Acts 23:1, 2; 2 Corinthians 11:24, 25.

Many will try to get us to do things that displease God. So the question is, How much do you love what is good? Do you love it so much that you will do what is good even when others hate you for it? It takes courage to do that, doesn't it?—

What did Paul suffer when he did what was good?

Why are these people trying to kill Jesus?

You may wonder, 'Why would people hate us for doing good? Shouldn't they be glad?' You would think so. Often people liked Jesus for the good things he did. Once, all the people of a city gathered at the door of the house where he was staying. They came because Jesus had been healing sick people.—Mark 1:33.

But sometimes people did not like what Jesus taught. Even though he always taught what was right, some showed real hatred for him because he spoke the truth. This happened one day in Nazareth, the city where Jesus grew up. He went into the synagogue, a place where Jewish people met to worship God.

There Jesus gave a fine talk from the Scriptures. The people liked it at first. They were amazed at the fine words that came out of his mouth. They could hardly believe that this was the young man who had grown up in their own city.

But then Jesus said something else. He told about times when God showed special favor to people who were not Jews. When Jesus said this, those in the synagogue became angry. Do you know why?— They thought that they were the only ones who had God's special favor. They thought that they were better than other people. So they hated Jesus for what he said. And do you know what they tried to do to him?—

The Bible says: 'They grabbed Jesus and rushed him outside the city. They led him to the edge of a mountain and were going to throw him over the cliff and kill him! But Jesus got away from them.'—Luke 4:16-30.

If that happened to you, would you ever go back to talk to those people about God?— That would take courage, wouldn't it?— Well, about a year later, Jesus did go back to Nazareth. The Bible says: "He began to teach them in their synagogue." Jesus did not stop speaking the truth because of fear of men who had no love for God.—Matthew 13:54.

On another day, a sabbath, Jesus was in a place where there was a man whose hand was withered, or crippled. Jesus had power from God to heal that man. But some of the men there were trying to make trouble for Jesus. What would the Great Teacher do?— First he asked: 'If you had a sheep that fell into a big hole on the Sabbath, would you lift it out?'

Yes, they would do that for a sheep, even on the Sabbath, the day when they were supposed to rest. So Jesus said: 'It is even better to help a man on the Sabbath, since a man is worth more than a sheep!' How clear it was that Jesus should help this man by healing him!

Jesus told the man to stretch out his hand. Right away it was made well. How happy that man was! But what about those other men? Were they glad?— No. They hated Jesus even more. They went out and made plans to kill him!—Matthew 12:9-14.

It is like that today. No matter what we do, we can never please everyone. So we have to decide whom we really want to please. If it is Jehovah God and his Son, Jesus Christ, then we must always do what they teach. But if we do, who will hate us? Who will make it hard for us to do what is good?—

Satan the Devil will. But who else will?— Those who have been fooled by the Devil into believing wrong things. Jesus told the religious leaders of his day: "You are from your father the Devil, and you wish to do the desires of your father."—John 8:44.

There are many people the Devil likes. Jesus calls them "the world." What do you think "the world" is that Jesus speaks about?— Well, let's look at John chapter 15, verse 19, and see. There we read these words of Jesus: "If you were part of the world, the world would be fond of what is its own. Now because you are no part of the world, but I have chosen you out of the world, on this account the world hates you."

So the world that hates Jesus' disciples is made up of all the people who are not his followers. Why does the world hate Jesus' disciples?— Think about it. Who is the ruler of the world?— The Bible says: "The whole world is lying in the power of the wicked one." That wicked one is Satan the Devil.—1 John 5:19.

Do you see now why it is so hard to do good?— Satan and his world make it hard. But there is another reason. Do you remember what it is?— In Chapter 23 of this book, we learned that we are all born with sin. Won't it be wonderful when sin, the Devil, and his world are gone?—

The Bible promises: "The world is passing away." This means that all of those who are not followers of the Great Teacher will be no more. They will not be allowed to live forever. Do you know who will live forever?— The Bible goes on to say: "He that does the will of God remains forever." (1 John 2:17) Yes, only those who do good, who do "the will of God," will live forever in God's new world. So even if it is hard, we want to do good, don't we?—

Let's read together these scriptures that show why it is not easy to do what is good: Matthew 7:13, 14; Luke 13:23, 24; and Acts 14:21, 22.

When this world passes away, what will happen to those who do good?

CHAPTER 27

WHO IS YOUR GOD?

WHY is the question, Who is your God? an important one?— Because people worship many gods. (1 Corinthians 8:5) When the apostle Paul received power from Jehovah to heal a man who had never walked before, the people cried out: "The gods have become like humans and have come down to us!" The people wanted to worship Paul and his friend Barnabas. They called Paul Hermes and Barnabas Zeus, which were the names of false gods.

But Paul and Barnabas would not let the people worship them. They leaped into the crowd and said: "Turn from these vain things to the living God." (Acts 14:8-15) Who is "the living God," who created all things?— Yes, he is Jehovah, "the Most High over all the earth." Jesus called Jehovah "the only true God." So, then, who alone deserves to be worshiped?— Only Jehovah!—Psalm 83:18; John 17:3; Revelation 4:11.

Most people worship gods other than "the only true God." They often worship things that they make from wood, stone, or metal. (Exodus 32:4-7; Leviticus 26:1; Isaiah 44:14-17) Even men and women who become famous are sometimes called gods, stars, or idols. Is it right to give glory to them?—

After Saul became the apostle Paul, he wrote: "The god of this system of things has blinded the minds of the unbelievers." (2 Corinthians 4:4) Who is this god?— Yes, Satan the Devil! Satan has been able to get people to worship many people and things.

Why didn't Paul and Barnabas let the people bow down to them?

When Satan tried to get Jesus to bow down and worship him, what did Jesus tell Satan?— "It is Jehovah your God you must worship, and *it is to him alone* you must render sacred service." (Matthew 4:10) So Jesus made it clear that worship belongs only to Jehovah. Let's read about some young men who knew this. Their names were Shadrach, Meshach, and Abednego.

These young Hebrews were part of God's nation of Israel and had been taken captive to the land of Babylon. There a king named Nebuchadnezzar built a huge image of gold. One day he commanded that when music was played, everyone should bow down to the image. 'Whoever does not bow down and worship will be thrown into the burning fiery furnace,' he warned. What would you have done?—

Why won't these men bow down to the image?

Usually, Shadrach, Meshach, and Abednego did everything that the king commanded. But they refused to do this. Do you know why?— It was because God's law said: 'You must not have any other gods besides me. You must not make for yourself a carved image and bow down to it.' (Exodus 20:3-5) So Shadrach, Meshach, and Abednego obeyed the law of Jehovah rather than the command of the king.

The king was very angry, so right away he had the three young Hebrews brought before him. He asked: 'Is it really so that, you are not serving my own gods? I will give you another chance. Now, when you hear the music, fall down and worship the image I have made. If you do not, you will be thrown into the burning fiery furnace. And who is that god that can rescue you out of my hands?'

What would the young men do now? What would you have done?— They said to the king: 'Our God whom we are serving is able to rescue us. But even if he does not do it, your gods are not the ones we will serve. We will not bow down to your image of gold.'

144

The king was furious. He commanded: 'Heat the furnace seven times hotter than usual!' He then ordered his strong men to tie up Shadrach, Meshach, and Abednego and throw them into the furnace! The furnace was so hot that the king's own men were killed by the flames! What about the three Hebrews?

Shadrach, Meshach, and Abednego fell right into the middle of the fire. But then they got up! They were not hurt. And they were no longer tied up. How could this be possible?— The king looked into the furnace, and what he saw made him afraid. 'Did we not throw three men into the fire?' he asked. His servants answered: "Yes, O king."

Then the king said: 'Look! I see four persons walking about in there, and the fire is not hurting any of them.' Do you know who that fourth person was?— It was Jehovah's angel. He protected the three Hebrews from getting hurt.

Well, on seeing this, the king came to the door of the furnace and cried out: "Shadrach, Meshach and

How did Jehovah save his servants from the fiery furnace?

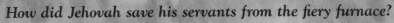

Abednego, you servants of the Most High God, step out and come here!" When they came out, everyone could see that they had not been burned. There was not even the smell of fire on them. Then the king said: 'Blessed be the God of Shadrach, Meshach and Abednego, who sent an angel to save his servants because they would not worship any god at all except their own God.'—Daniel, chapter 3.

We can learn a lesson from what happened back then. Even today men set up images, or idols, for worship. *The Encyclopedia Americana* says: "The flag, like the cross, is sacred." Images can be made of wood, stone, metal, or cloth. Early disciples of Jesus would not do an act of worship to the Roman emperor, which the historian Daniel P. Mannix said could be compared with "refusing to salute the flag or repeat the oath of allegiance."

What idols do people give glory to today?

So do you think it makes a difference to God if a religious image is made out of cloth, wood, stone, or metal?— Would it be right for a servant of Jehovah to do an act of worship before such an image?— Shadrach, Meshach, and Abednego wouldn't do it, and Jehovah was pleased with them. How can you copy their example?—

Those who serve Jehovah cannot worship any other person or thing. Read what is said about this at Joshua 24:14, 15, 19-22; Isaiah 42:8; 1 John 5:21; and Revelation 19:10.

CHAPTER 28

HOW TO KNOW
WHOM TO OBEY

SOMETIMES it is hard to know whom we should obey. Your mother or father may tell you to do one thing. But then a schoolteacher or a policeman may tell you to do something different. If that happened, which one of them would you obey?—

Earlier in this book, in Chapter 7, we read Ephesians 6:1-3 from the Bible. There it says that children should obey their parents. "Be obedient to your parents *in union with the Lord*," the scripture says. Do you know what it means to be *"in union with the Lord"*?— Parents who are *in union with the Lord* teach their children to obey God's laws.

But some older people do not believe in Jehovah. So, what if one of them says that it is all right to cheat on a school test or to take something from a store without paying for it? Is it all right, then, for a child to cheat or steal?—

Remember, King Nebuchadnezzar once commanded everyone to bow down to the golden image he had set up. But Shadrach, Meshach, and Abednego wouldn't bow down. Do you know why?— Because the Bible says that people should worship only Jehovah.—Exodus 20:3; Matthew 4:10.

After Jesus died, his apostles were brought before the Sanhedrin, the main religious court of the Jews. High Priest Caiaphas said: "We positively ordered you not to keep teaching upon the basis of [Jesus'] name, and yet, look! you have filled Jerusalem with your teaching." Why didn't the apostles obey the Sanhedrin?— Peter, speaking for all the apostles, answered Caiaphas: "We must obey God as ruler rather than men."—Acts 5: 27-29.

What is Peter saying to Caiaphas?

Back at that time, the religious leaders of the Jews had a lot of power. However, their country was under the rule of the Roman government. The head of that government was called Caesar. Even though the Jews did not want Caesar to rule them, the Roman government did many good things for the people. And governments today also do good things for their citizens. Do you know what some of these things are?—

Governments build roads for travel and pay policemen and firemen to protect us. They may also provide schooling for the young and health care for the elderly. It costs money for a government to do these things. Do you know where the government gets the money?— From the people. The money that people pay to the government is called taxes.

When the Great Teacher lived on earth, many Jews did not want to pay taxes to the Roman government. So one day the priests hired some men to ask Jesus a question to try to get him into trouble. The question was, 'Do we have to pay tax to Caesar or not?' This was a trick question. If Jesus answered, 'Yes, you must pay taxes,' many of the Jews would not like what he said. But Jesus could not say, 'No, you don't need to pay taxes.' It would be wrong to say that.

So, what did Jesus do? Well, he said: 'Show me a coin.' When they brought him one, Jesus asked them: 'Whose picture and name are on it?' The men said: "Caesar's." So Jesus said: "By all means, then, pay back Caesar's things to Caesar, but God's things to God."—Luke 20:19-26.

Well, no one could find anything wrong with that answer. If Caesar does things for people, it is only right to use the money that Caesar has made to pay him for these things. So in this way, Jesus showed that it is right to pay taxes to the government for the things we receive.

How did Jesus answer the trick question of these men?

Now, you may not be old enough to pay taxes. But there is something that you should give to the government. Do you know what it is?— Obedience to the government's laws. The Bible says: 'Be obedient to the superior authorities.' These authorities are those who have power in the government. So God is the one who says that we should obey the laws of the government.—Romans 13:1, 2.

There may be a law not to throw paper or other things on the street. Should you obey that law?— Yes, God wants you to obey it. Should you be obedient to policemen too?— The government pays policemen to protect people. Obeying them is the same as obeying the government.

So if you are about to cross a street and a policeman says "Wait!" what should you do?— If others run across anyway, should you?— You should wait, even if you are the only one who is waiting. God tells you to obey.

There may be trouble in the neighborhood, and a policeman may say: "Stay off the streets. Don't go outside." But you may hear shouting and wonder what's going on. Should you go outside to see?— Would this be obeying "the superior authorities"?—

In many places, the government also builds schools, and it pays the teachers. So do you think that God wants you to obey the teacher?— Think about it. The government pays the teacher to teach, just as it pays a policeman to protect people. So being obedient to either a policeman or a teacher is like obeying the government.

Why should we obey a policeman?

But what if a teacher says that you must do an act of worship to some image? What would you do then?— The three Hebrews did not bow down to the image, even when King Nebuchadnezzar told them to. Do you remember why?— Because they did not want to disobey God.

A history writer named Will Durant wrote about the early Christians and said that their 'highest allegiance [or, loyalty] did not belong to Caesar.' No, it belonged to Jehovah! So remember that God should come first in our lives.

We obey the government because that is what God wants us to do. But if we are told to do something that God says we should not do, what should we say?— We should say what the apostles said to the high priest: "We must obey God as ruler rather than men."—Acts 5:29.

Respect for the law is taught in the Bible. Read what is written at Matthew 5:41; Titus 3:1; and 1 Peter 2:12-14.

CHAPTER 29

DO ALL PARTIES PLEASE GOD?

DO YOU like to have parties?— They can be lots of fun. Do you think the Great Teacher would want us to go to parties?— Well, he went to what could be called a party when someone got married, and some of his disciples went with him. Jehovah is "the happy God," so he is pleased when we enjoy ourselves at good parties. —1 Timothy 1:11; John 2:1-11.

Page 29 of this book tells us that Jehovah parted the Red Sea to let the Israelites pass through. Do you remember reading that?— Afterward, the people sang and danced and gave thanks to Jehovah. It was like a party. The people were very happy, and we can be sure that God was happy too.—Exodus 15:1, 20, 21.

Nearly 40 years later, the Israelites went to another big party. This time the people who invited them did not even worship Jehovah. In fact, the people who invited them even bowed down to worship other gods and would have sex relations with people they were not married to. Do you think it was all right to go to a party like that?— Well, Jehovah was not pleased, and he punished the Israelites. —Numbers 25:1-9; 1 Corinthians 10:8.

Why was God pleased with this party?

The Bible also tells about two birthday parties. Was one of them to celebrate the birthday of the Great Teacher?— No. Both of these birthday parties were for men who did not serve Jehovah. One was the birthday party for King Herod Antipas. He was the ruler of the district of Galilee when Jesus lived there.

King Herod did many bad things. He took the wife of his brother for himself. Her name was Herodias. God's servant John the Baptist told Herod that it was wrong for him to do that. Herod did not like that. So he had John locked up in prison.—Luke 3:19, 20.

While John was in prison, the day came for celebrating Herod's birth. Herod gave a big party. He invited many important people. They all ate and drank and enjoyed themselves. Then the daughter of Herodias came in and danced for them. Everyone was so pleased with her dancing that King Herod wanted to give her a special gift. He said to her: "Whatever you ask me for, I will give it to you, up to half my kingdom."

What happened at Herod's birthday party?

153

What would she ask for? Would it be money? pretty clothes? a palace of her own? The girl did not know what to say. So she went to her mother, Herodias, and said: "What should I ask for?"

Now Herodias hated John the Baptist very much. So she told her daughter to ask for his head. The girl went back to the king and said: "I want you to give me right away on a platter the head of John the Baptist."

King Herod did not want to kill John because he knew that John was a good man. But Herod had made a promise, and he was afraid of what others at the party would think if he changed his mind. So he sent a man to the prison to chop off the head of John. Soon the man came back. He had John's head on a platter, and he gave it to the girl. Then the girl gave it to her mother. —Mark 6:17-29.

The other birthday party that the Bible tells about wasn't any better. It was for a king of Egypt. During this party also, the king had someone's head chopped off. Then, after

Why could Jesus' birth not have been on December 25?

that, he hung the man up for the birds to eat! (Genesis 40:19-22) Do you think that God approved of those two parties?— Would you have wanted to be at them?—

We know that everything in the Bible is there for a reason. It tells about just two birthday parties. And at both of them, bad things were done as part of the celebration. So, what would you say that God is telling us about birthday parties? Does God want us to celebrate birthdays?—

It is true that at such parties today, people do not chop off someone's head. But the whole idea of celebrating birthdays started with people who did not worship the true God. *The Catholic Encyclopedia* says about the birthday celebrations mentioned in the Bible: "Only sinners . . . make great rejoicings over the day on which they were born." Do we want to be like them?—

What about the Great Teacher? Did he celebrate his birthday?— No, the Bible does not say anything about a birthday party for Jesus. In fact, Jesus' early followers did not celebrate his birthday. Do you know why people later chose to celebrate Jesus' birthday on December 25?—

That date was chosen because, as *The World Book Encyclopedia* says, "the people of Rome already observed it as the Feast of Saturn, celebrating the birthday of the sun." So people chose to celebrate Jesus' birthday on a date when pagans already had a holiday!

Do you know why Jesus could not have been born in December?— Because the Bible says that when Jesus was born, shepherds were still in the fields at night. (Luke 2:8-12) And they would not have been out there in the cold, rainy month of December.

Many people know that Christmas is not the birthday of Jesus. They even know that on that day pagans had a celebration that was not pleasing to God. But many celebrate Christmas anyway. They are more concerned with having a party than with finding out what God really thinks about it. But we want to please Jehovah, don't we?—

So when we have parties, we want to make sure that they are good ones in Jehovah's eyes. We can have them anytime during the year. We don't have to wait for a special day. We can eat some special food and have fun playing games. Would you like to do that?— Maybe you can talk with your parents and plan a party with their help. That would be nice, wouldn't it?— But before you make the plans for a party, you want to make sure it is something that God would approve.

The importance of always doing what God approves is also shown at Proverbs 12:2; John 8:29; Romans 12:2; and 1 John 3:22.

How can we make sure our parties are pleasing to God?

CHAPTER 30

HELP TO OVERCOME OUR FEARS

DO YOU find it easy to serve Jehovah?— The Great Teacher didn't say it would be easy to do. The night before Jesus was killed, he told his apostles: "If the world hates you, you know that it has hated me before it hated you." —John 15:18.

Peter bragged that he would never leave Jesus, but Jesus said that Peter would deny knowing him three times that very night. And this is exactly what Peter did! (Matthew 26:31-35, 69-75) How could such a thing happen?— It happened because Peter became afraid, and so did the other apostles.

Do you know why the apostles became afraid?— They had failed to do something very important. Learning about this can help us to serve Jehovah, no matter what anyone may say or do to us. To begin with, though, we need to review what happened on the last night that Jesus spent with his apostles.

First, they celebrate the Passover together. This was a special meal held every year to remind God's people of their deliverance from slavery in Egypt. Then Jesus introduces another special meal with them. We will discuss it in a later chapter and explain how that meal helps us to remember Jesus. After that meal and after words of encouragement to his apostles, Jesus takes them out to the garden of Gethsemane. This is a favorite place they have often visited.

Jesus goes off by himself in the garden to pray. He also tells Peter, James, and John to pray. But they fall asleep. Three times Jesus goes away by himself to pray, and three times he comes back to find Peter and the others sleeping! (Matthew 26:36-47) Do you know why they should have stayed awake to pray?— Let's talk about this.

Judas Iscariot was at the Passover with Jesus and the other apostles earlier that evening. As you may remember, Judas had become a thief. Now he becomes a traitor. He knows about the place in the garden of Gethsemane where Jesus has often met together with his apostles. So Judas brings soldiers there to arrest Jesus. When they arrive, Jesus asks them: "Whom are you looking for?"

The soldiers reply: "Jesus." Jesus is not afraid, so he answers: "I am he." The soldiers are so surprised by Jesus' courage that they draw back and fall to the ground. Then Jesus says: 'If it is I you are looking for, let my apostles go.'—John 18:1-9.

When the soldiers grab Jesus and tie him up, the apostles become afraid and run away. But Peter and John want to find out what happens, so they follow at a distance. Eventually, Jesus is brought to the home of Caiaphas, the high priest. Since John is known to the high priest, the gatekeeper lets him and Peter into the courtyard.

The priests have already come together at the home of Caiaphas to have a trial. They want to have Jesus put to death. So they bring in witnesses who tell lies about him. The people hit Jesus with their fists and slap him. While all of this is happening, Peter is nearby.

Why should Peter, James, and John have stayed awake?

A servant girl, the gatekeeper who let Peter and John in, notices Peter. "You, too, were with Jesus!" she says. But Peter denies even knowing Jesus. After a while another girl recognizes Peter and says to those standing by: "This man was with Jesus." Again Peter denies knowing him. Sometime later a group of people see Peter and say to him: "Certainly you also are one of them." For the third time Peter denies it, saying: "I do not know the man!" Peter even swears that he is telling the truth, and Jesus turns and looks at him.—Matthew 26:57-75; Luke 22:54-62; John 18:15-27.

Do you know why Peter lied?— Yes, because he was afraid. But why was he afraid? What had he failed to do to build up his courage? Think about it. What had Jesus done to gain courage?— He had prayed to God, and God helped him to have courage. And remember, Jesus had told Peter three times to pray and to stay awake and to keep on the watch. But what had happened?—

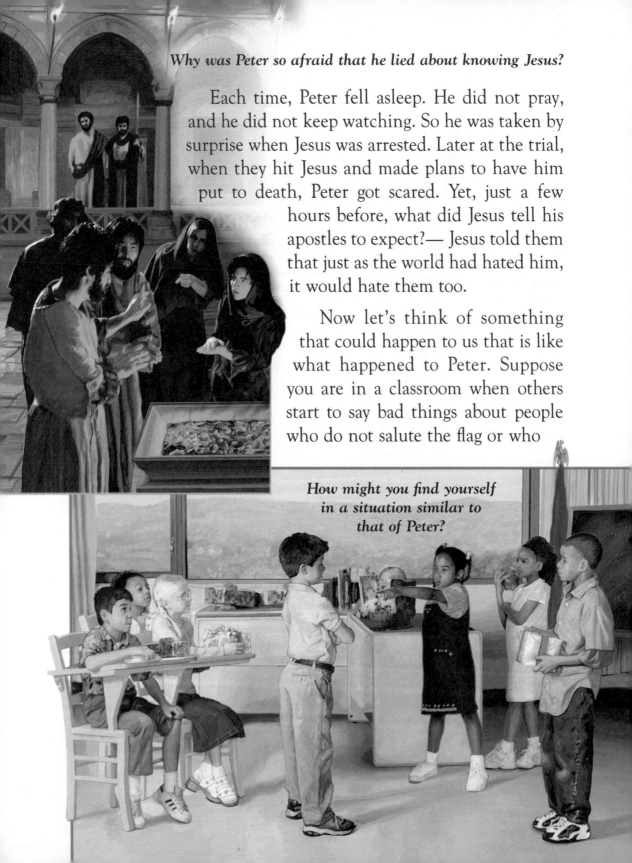

Why was Peter so afraid that he lied about knowing Jesus?

Each time, Peter fell asleep. He did not pray, and he did not keep watching. So he was taken by surprise when Jesus was arrested. Later at the trial, when they hit Jesus and made plans to have him put to death, Peter got scared. Yet, just a few hours before, what did Jesus tell his apostles to expect?— Jesus told them that just as the world had hated him, it would hate them too.

Now let's think of something that could happen to us that is like what happened to Peter. Suppose you are in a classroom when others start to say bad things about people who do not salute the flag or who

How might you find yourself in a situation similar to that of Peter?

do not celebrate Christmas. Then what if someone turns to you and asks: "Is it true *you* don't salute the flag?" Or others say: "We hear you don't even celebrate Christmas!" Would you be afraid to tell the truth?— Would you be tempted to lie, as Peter did?—

Afterward, Peter was very sorry that he had denied knowing Jesus. When he realized what he had done, he went outside and cried. Yes, he returned to Jesus. (Luke 22:32) Now think about it. What can help us not to become so afraid that we say something like Peter did?— Remember, Peter had failed to pray and to keep on the watch. So, what would you say that we need to do to be a follower of the Great Teacher?—

We certainly need to pray to Jehovah for help. When Jesus prayed, do you know what God did for him?— He sent an angel to strengthen him. (Luke 22:43) Can God's angels help us?— The Bible says: "The angel of Jehovah is camping all around those fearing him, and he rescues them." (Psalm 34:7) But to receive God's help, we need to do more than pray for it. Do you know what else we need to do?— Jesus told his followers to stay awake and keep on the watch. How would you say we can do that?—

We need to listen carefully to what is said at our Christian meetings and to pay attention to what we read from the Bible. But we also need to pray to Jehovah regularly and to ask him to help us serve him. If we do, we will receive help to overcome our fears. Then we will be glad when we have an opportunity to tell others about the Great Teacher and his Father.

These scriptures can help us never to let fear of other people hold us back from doing what is right: Proverbs 29:25; Jeremiah 26:12-15, 20-24; and John 12:42, 43.

CHAPTER 31

WHERE TO FIND COMFORT

DO YOU ever feel sad and lonely?— Do you ever wonder if anybody loves you?— Some children do. But God promises: "*I myself shall not forget you.*" (Isaiah 49:15) Isn't that wonderful to think about?— Yes, Jehovah God really does love us!

One Bible writer said: "In case my own father and my own mother did leave me, even Jehovah himself would take me up." (Psalm 27:10) Knowing that can be a real comfort to us, can't it?— Yes, Jehovah tells us: "Do not be afraid, for I am with you. . . . *I will really help you.*"—Isaiah 41:10.

Sometimes, though, Jehovah lets Satan make trouble for us. Jehovah even lets Satan test His servants. The Devil once made Jesus suffer so much that Jesus cried out to Jehovah: 'My God, my God, why have you left me?' (Matthew 27:46) Even though Jesus was suffering, he still knew that Jehovah loved him. (John 10:17) But Jesus also knew that God lets Satan test His servants and allows Satan to cause them to suffer. In another chapter we will explain why God lets Satan do this.

When we are little, it is hard not to be afraid sometimes. For example, have you ever been lost?— Were you scared?— Many children would be. The Great Teacher once told a story about one that was lost. But it was not a child who was lost. It was a sheep.

In some ways you are like a sheep. How is that? Well, sheep are not very big or strong. And they need someone to take

care of them and to protect them. The man who takes care of sheep is called a shepherd.

In his story Jesus told about a shepherd who had a hundred sheep. But then one of the sheep got lost. It may have wanted to see what was on the other side of the hill. But before long, that sheep was far away from the others. Can you imagine how that sheep felt when it looked around and saw that it was all alone?—

What would the shepherd do when he found that the one sheep was missing? Would he say that this was all the sheep's fault anyway so he wasn't going to worry about it? Or would he leave the 99 sheep in a safe place and go looking for just the one? Would one sheep be worth that much trouble?— If you were that lost sheep, would you want the shepherd to look for you?—

The shepherd loved all his sheep very much, even the one that was lost. So he went in search of the missing one. Think of how glad that lost sheep was when it saw the shepherd coming! And Jesus said that the shepherd rejoiced that he had found his sheep. He rejoiced over it more than over the 99 sheep that had not got lost. Now, who is like that shepherd in Jesus' story? Who cares for us as much as that shepherd did for his sheep?— Jesus said that his Father in heaven does. And his Father is Jehovah.

Jehovah God is the Great Shepherd of his people. He loves all of those who serve him, including young ones like you. He does not want any of us to be hurt or destroyed. Surely it is wonderful to know that God cares for us that much!—Matthew 18:12-14.

Do you really believe in Jehovah God?— Is he a real person to you?— It is true that we cannot see Jehovah. This is because he is a Spirit. He has a body that is invisible to our eyes.

Who is like the shepherd that has rescued his sheep?

But he is a real person, and he can see us. He knows when we need help. And we can talk to him in prayer, just as we talk to another person on earth. Jehovah wants us to do this.

So if you ever feel sad or all alone, what should you do?—Talk to Jehovah. Draw close to him, and he will comfort and help you. Remember that Jehovah loves you, even when you feel as if you are all alone. Let's get our Bible. Here in Psalm 23, we are told, beginning at verse 1: "Jehovah is my Shepherd. I shall lack nothing. In grassy pastures he makes me lie down; by well-watered resting-places he conducts me."

Notice what the writer adds, in verse 4: "Even though I walk in the valley of deep shadow, I fear nothing bad, for you are with me; your rod and your staff are the things that comfort me." That's the way people feel if their God is Jehovah. They find comfort when they are in trouble. Is that the way you feel?—

Is Jehovah as real to you as your father or some other person is?

As a loving shepherd takes care of his flock, so Jehovah takes good care of his people. He shows them the right way to go, and they gladly follow him. Even when there is trouble all around them, they do not need to be afraid. A shepherd uses his rod or his staff to protect the sheep from animals that might harm them. The Bible tells about how the young shepherd David protected his sheep from a lion and a bear. (1 Samuel 17:34-36) And God's people know that Jehovah will protect them too. They can feel safe because God is with them.

Jehovah really loves his sheep, and he tenderly cares for them. The Bible says: 'Like a shepherd he will lead his own sheep. With his arms he will collect the little ones together. The young ones he will help along with care.'—Isaiah 40:11.

Doesn't it make you feel good to know that Jehovah is like that?— Do you want to be one of his sheep?— Sheep listen to the voice of their shepherd. They stay close to him. Do you listen to Jehovah?— Do you stay close to him?— Then you never need to be afraid. Jehovah will be with you.

Jehovah lovingly cares for those who serve him. Let's read together what the Bible says about this, at Psalm 37:25 (36:25, "Dy"); 55:22 (54:23, "Dy"); and Luke 12:29-31.

Like a shepherd protecting his sheep, who can help us when we are in trouble?

CHAPTER 32

HOW JESUS WAS PROTECTED

JEHOVAH sometimes does things in a wonderful way to protect those who are young and who are unable to protect themselves. If you go walking in the country, you may see one way that Jehovah does this. But at first you may not really understand what is happening.

You see a bird land on the ground near you. It seems to be hurt. It drags one of its wings and moves away when you try to approach it. As you follow the bird, it keeps just ahead of you. Then, suddenly, the bird flies away. Its wing was not hurt at all! Do you know what the bird was doing?—

Well, close to where the bird landed near you, its babies were hidden in the bushes. The mother bird was afraid that you might find them and hurt them. So she pretended to be hurt and led you away. Do you know who can protect us as a mother bird does her babies?— In the Bible, Jehovah is compared to a bird called an eagle, which helps its little ones. —Deuteronomy 32:11, 12.

How is this mother bird protecting her little ones?

167

The most precious child of Jehovah is his dear Son, Jesus. When Jesus was in heaven, he was a powerful spirit person like his Father. He could take care of himself. But when Jesus was born as a baby on earth, he was helpless. He needed protection.

To fulfill God's will for him on earth, Jesus had to grow up and become a perfect, full-grown man. Satan, however, tried to kill Jesus before that could happen. The attempts to kill Jesus when he was a child and the ways Jehovah protected him make an exciting story. Would you like to hear it?—

A short time after Jesus is born, Satan causes what appears to be a star to shine in the sky in the East. Men called astrologers, who study the stars, follow the star hundreds of miles to Jerusalem. There they ask where the one to be king of the Jews is to be born. When men who know what the Bible says about this are asked, they answer: "In Bethlehem."—Matthew 2:1-6.

After the astrologers visit Jesus, what warning does God give them that saves Jesus?

After Herod, the bad king in Jerusalem, hears about this new king who has recently been born in the nearby town of Bethlehem, he tells the astrologers: 'Search and find the child, and then come back and tell me.' Do you know why Herod wants to know where to find Jesus?— It is because Herod is jealous and wants to kill him!

How does God protect his Son?— Well, when the astrologers find Jesus, they give him gifts. Later God gives the astrologers a warning in a dream not to return to Herod. So they go home another way without returning to Jerusalem. When Herod finds out that the astrologers have left, he is very angry. In an effort to kill Jesus, Herod has all the boys in Bethlehem under two years of age killed! But by then, Jesus is gone.

Do you know how Jesus escapes?— After the astrologers leave to go home, Jehovah gives a warning to Mary's husband, Joseph, to get up and run far away to Egypt. There Jesus is safe from bad Herod. Years later, when Mary and Joseph return from Egypt with Jesus, God gives another warning to Joseph. He tells him in a dream to move to Nazareth, where Jesus will be safe. —Matthew 2:7-23.

How is young Jesus saved again?

Do you see how Jehovah protected his Son?— Who would you say is like the little birds hidden by their mother in the bushes or like Jesus when he was a small child? Aren't you like them?— There are those who want to hurt you too. Do you know who?—

The Bible says that Satan is like a roaring lion who wants to eat us. And just as lions often pick on small animals, Satan and his demons often pick on children. (1 Peter 5:8) But Jehovah is stronger than Satan. Jehovah can protect his children or undo anything bad that Satan does to them.

Do you remember from Chapter 10 of this book what the Devil and his demons try to get us to do?— Yes, they try to get us to have the kind of sex relations that God says is wrong. But who only should have sex relations?— Yes, two grown people of the opposite sex who are married to each other.

However, sad to say, some grown-ups like to have sex with children. When they do, boys and girls may begin to do bad things that they have learned from these grown-ups. They also begin to use their sex organs in a wrong way. That is what happened a long time ago in the city of Sodom. The Bible says that people there, *"from boy* to old man," tried to have sex with men who had come to visit Lot.—Genesis 19:4, 5.

So just as Jesus needed protection, you also need to be protected from grown-ups—and even from other children—who may try to have sex with you. Usually, these people will pretend to be your friends. They may even offer you something if you will promise not to tell others about what they want to do with you. But these people are selfish, like Satan and his demons, and they only want to get pleasure for themselves. And they try to get this pleasure by having sex with children. *This is very wrong!*

What should you say and do if someone tries to touch you in a wrong way?

Do you know what they may do to get pleasure for themselves?— Well, they may try to rub your sex organs. Or they will even rub their sex organs against yours. But you should never let anybody play with your penis or vulva. Not even your own brother or sister or your mother or father. *These parts of your body are private.*

How can you protect your body from people who do bad things like this?— First of all, do not let anybody play with your sex organs. If someone tries to do this, say firmly in a loud voice: *"Stop that! I'm going to tell on you!"* And if that person says that what happened is your fault, don't believe that. It is not true. Just go and tell on him no matter who it is! You should do so even if he says that what you are doing together is a secret just between you and him. Even if that person promises you nice presents or makes scary threats, you should get away from him and tell on him anyway.

You do not have to be afraid, but you do need to be careful. When your parents warn you about people or places that could be a danger to you, you need to listen to them. If you do, you take away a bad person's chance to hurt you.

Read about protecting yourself from wrong sex acts, at Genesis 39:7-12; Proverbs 4:14-16; 14:15, 16; 1 Corinthians 6:18; and 2 Peter 2:14.

CHAPTER 33

JESUS CAN PROTECT US

WHEN Jesus grew older and learned how he had been protected when he was little, do you think that he prayed to Jehovah and thanked him?— What do you think Jesus may later have told Mary and Joseph when he learned that they had saved his life by taking him to Egypt?—

Of course, Jesus is not a baby anymore. He isn't even living on earth as he once did. But have you noticed that now some people seem to think of Jesus only as a baby in a manger?— This is true at Christmastime when in many places pictures are seen of Jesus as a baby.

Even though Jesus is no longer living on earth, do you believe he is alive?— Yes, he was raised from the dead, and he is now a powerful King in heaven. What do you think he can do to protect those who serve him?— Well, when Jesus was on earth, he showed how he could protect those who loved him. Let's see how he did that one day when he was out in a boat with his disciples.

How do you view Jesus—as a powerful King or a helpless baby?

It is late in the afternoon. Jesus has been teaching all day by the Sea of Galilee, which is a large lake about 13 miles long and 7.5 miles wide. Now he says to his disciples: "Let us cross to the other side of the lake." So they set out in a boat and start to sail across the lake. Jesus is very tired, so he goes to the back of the boat and lies down on a pillow. Soon he is fast asleep.

The disciples stay awake to keep the boat on its course. Everything is all right for a while, but then a strong wind springs up. It blows harder and harder, and the waves keep getting bigger. The waves begin splashing into the boat, and the boat starts to fill up with water.

The disciples are afraid that they are going to sink. But Jesus is not afraid. He is still asleep in the back of the boat. Finally, the disciples wake him, and say: 'Teacher, Teacher, save us; we are about to die in this storm.' At that, Jesus gets up and speaks to the wind and the waves. "Hush! Be quiet!" he says.

What is Jesus saying to the wind and the waves?

Right away the wind stops blowing, and the lake becomes calm. The disciples are amazed. They have never seen anything like it before. They begin saying to one another: "Who really is this, for he orders even the winds and the water, and they obey him?"—Luke 8:22-25; Mark 4:35-41.

Do you know who Jesus is?— Do you know where he gets his great power?— The disciples should not have been afraid when Jesus was there with them, for Jesus was no ordinary man. He could do wonderful things that no other person could do. Let me tell you about something else that he once did on a stormy sea.

Why did Jesus perform miracles?

It is sometime later, on another day. When it becomes evening, Jesus tells his disciples to board a boat and go ahead of him to the other side of the sea. Then Jesus goes up into the mountain by himself. It is a quiet place where he can pray to his Father, Jehovah God.

The disciples get into the boat and start to sail across the sea. But soon a wind begins to blow. It blows harder and harder. It is now nighttime. The men take down the sail and begin to row. But they are not getting very far because the strong wind is blowing against them. The boat is rocking back and forth in the high waves, and water is splashing in. The men work hard trying to reach shore, but they cannot.

Jesus is still alone in the mountain. He has been there a long time. But now he can see that his disciples are in danger in the high waves. So he comes down from the mountain to the edge of the sea. Jesus wants to help his disciples, so he starts walking toward them over the stormy sea!

What would happen if you tried to walk on water?— You would sink, and you might drown. But Jesus is different. He has special power. Jesus has a long walk to reach the boat. So it is about dawn when the disciples see Jesus coming toward them over the water. But they can't believe what they see. They are very frightened, and they cry out in their fear. Then Jesus speaks to them: "Take courage, it is I; have no fear."

As soon as Jesus gets up into the boat, the storm stops. The disciples are again amazed. They fall down before Jesus and say: "You are really God's Son."—Matthew 14:22-33; John 6:16-21.

Wouldn't it have been wonderful to live back then and to see Jesus do things like that?— Do you know why Jesus did those miraculous things?— He did those things because he loved his disciples and wanted to help them. But he also did those things to show the great power that he had and would use in the future as the Ruler of God's Kingdom.

Even today Jesus often uses his power to protect his followers from Satan's efforts to stop them from telling others about God's Kingdom. But Jesus does not use his power to protect his disciples from getting sick or to cure them when they are sick. Even all of Jesus' apostles eventually died. John's brother James was murdered, and John himself was put in prison. —Acts 12:2; Revelation 1:9.

It is similar today. Whether people serve Jehovah or not, they all can get sick and die. But soon, during the rule of Jesus as King of God's government, things will be different. No one then will ever have to be afraid, because Jesus will use his power for the blessing of all who obey him.—Isaiah 9:6, 7.

How does Jesus protect his followers today?

Other texts that show the great power of Jesus, the one whom God makes Ruler in the Kingdom of God, are Daniel 7:13, 14; Matthew 28:18; and Ephesians 1:20-22.

CHAPTER 34

WHAT WILL HAPPEN
IF WE DIE?

AS YOU may well know, people today grow old, get sick, and die. Even some children die. Should you be afraid of death or of anybody who has died?— Do you know what happens if we die?—

Well, nobody living today has been dead and come back to life to tell us about it. But when Jesus, the Great Teacher, was on earth, there was such a man. We can learn about what happens to those who die by reading about him. The man was a friend of Jesus and lived in Bethany, a small town not far from Jerusalem. His name was Lazarus, and he had two sisters, named Martha and Mary. Let's see what the Bible says happened.

One day Lazarus gets very sick. At the time, Jesus is far away. So Martha and Mary send a messenger to tell Jesus that their brother, Lazarus, is sick. They do this because they know that Jesus can come and make their brother well. Jesus is not a doctor, but he has power from God so that he can cure every kind of sickness.—Matthew 15:30, 31.

Before Jesus goes to see Lazarus, however, Lazarus gets so sick that he dies. But Jesus tells his disciples that Lazarus is sleeping and that He will go to wake him up. The disciples do not understand what Jesus means. So Jesus says plainly: "Lazarus has died." What does this show about death?— Yes, that it is like a deep sleep. It is a sleep so deep that the person does not even dream.

Jesus is now coming to visit Martha and Mary. Many friends of the family have already arrived. They have come to comfort the sisters because their brother has died. When Martha hears that Jesus is coming, she goes to meet him. Soon Mary also goes out to see Jesus. She is very sad and is crying, and she falls at his feet. Other friends who have followed Mary are also crying.

The Great Teacher asks where they have put Lazarus. At that, the people lead Jesus to the cave where Lazarus has been buried. When Jesus sees all the people crying, he starts to cry too. He knows how painful it is to lose a loved one in death.

A stone is in front of the cave, so Jesus says: "Take the stone away." Should they do it?— Martha does not think it is a good idea. She says: "Lord, by now he must smell, for it is four days."

But Jesus says to her: "Did I not tell you that if you would believe you would see the glory of God?" Jesus means that Martha would see something that would bring honor to God. What is Jesus going to do? When the stone is removed, Jesus prays out loud to Jehovah. Then Jesus says in a loud voice: "Lazarus, come on out!" Would he come out? Could he?—

Well, can you wake up somebody who is sleeping?— Yes, if you call in a loud voice, he will wake up. But can you wake up someone who is sleeping in death?— No. No matter how loud you call, the one who is dead will not hear. There is nothing that you or I or any other person on earth today can do to wake the dead.

But Jesus is different. He has special power from God. So when Jesus calls Lazarus, an amazing thing happens. The man who has been dead for four days comes out of the cave! He is brought back to life! He can breathe and walk and speak again! Yes, Jesus raises Lazarus from the dead.—John 11:1-44.

What has Jesus done for Lazarus?

Now think about it: What happened to Lazarus when he died? Did some part of him—a soul or a spirit—leave his body and go to live somewhere else? Did Lazarus' soul go to heaven? Was he alive for four days up there with God and the holy angels?—

No, he wasn't. Remember, Jesus said Lazarus was sleeping. What is it like when you are asleep? When you are in a very deep sleep, you do not know what is going on around you, do you?— And when you wake up, you do not know how long you have been sleeping until you look at a clock.

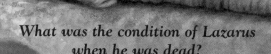

What was the condition of Lazarus when he was dead?

It is like that with dead people. They do not *know* anything. They do not *feel* anything. And they cannot *do* anything. That is the way it was with Lazarus when he was dead. Death is like a deep sleep where a person doesn't remember anything. The Bible says: "As for the dead, they are conscious of nothing at all."—Ecclesiastes 9:5, 10.

Think about this too: If Lazarus had been in heaven for those four days, would he not have said something about it?— And if he had been in heaven, would Jesus have made him come back to earth from that wonderful place?— Of course not!

Yet, many people say that we *have* a soul, and they say that the soul lives on after the body dies. They say that Lazarus' soul was alive somewhere. But the Bible does not say that. It says that God made the first man Adam "a living soul." Adam *was* a soul. The Bible also says that when Adam sinned, he died. He became a "dead soul," and he returned to the dust from which he had been made. The Bible also says that all Adam's offspring inherited sin and death too.—Genesis 2:7; 3:17-19; Numbers 6:6; Romans 5:12.

Clearly, then, we do not *have* a soul that is separate from our body. Each one of us *is* a soul. And since people have inherited sin from the first man, Adam, the Bible says: 'The soul that sins will die.'—Ezekiel 18:4.

Some people are afraid of the dead. They won't go near a graveyard because they think that the dead have souls separate from their body that could harm the living. But can a dead person harm someone who is alive?— No, he can't.

Some people even believe that the dead can come back as spirits to visit the living. So they set out food for the dead. But people who do that do not really believe what God says about the dead. If we believe what God says, we won't be afraid of the dead. And if we are really thankful to God for life, we will show it by doing things that God approves.

But you may wonder: 'Will God bring children who have died back to life? Does he really *want* to?' Let's talk about that next.

Let's read further in the Bible about the condition of the dead and about man being a soul, at Psalm 115:17 (113:17, "Dy"); 146:3, 4 (145:3, 4, "Dy"); and Jeremiah 2:34.

Why is there no reason to be afraid of the dead?

CHAPTER 35

WE CAN WAKE UP FROM DEATH!

IF WE die, will God *want* to resurrect us, that is, bring us back to life?— The good man Job believed that God wanted to. So when Job thought he was about to die, he said to God: "You will call, and I myself shall answer you." Job said that Jehovah God would *yearn*, or want very much, to resurrect him.—Job 14:14, 15.

Jesus is just like Jehovah God, his Father. Jesus *wants* to help us. When a man sick with leprosy said to him, "if you just *want to*, you can make me clean," Jesus answered: *"I want to."* And he healed the sick man from his leprosy.—Mark 1:40-42.

Jesus learned from his Father to have love for children. On two occasions long ago, Jehovah used his servants to resurrect little ones. Elijah begged Jehovah to resurrect the son of a woman who had been nice to Elijah. And Jehovah did it. Jehovah

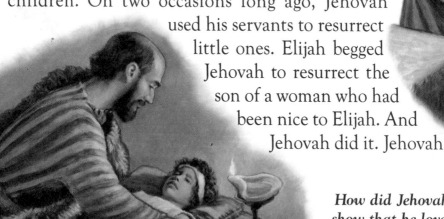

How did Jehovah show that he loves little ones?

also used his servant Elisha to resurrect a small boy.—1 Kings 17:17-24; 2 Kings 4:32-37.

Isn't it wonderful to know that Jehovah loves us so much?— He doesn't think of us just when we are alive. He also remembers us if we should die. Jesus said that the Father even considers dead ones whom he loves to be alive! (Luke 20:38) The Bible says that 'neither death nor life nor things here nor things to come will be able to separate us from God's love.' —Romans 8:38, 39.

When Jesus was on earth, he showed that Jehovah cares for little children. You will remember that Jesus took time to talk to children about God. But did you know that God gave Jesus the power to bring young ones back from the dead?— Let's talk about the time Jesus resurrected the 12-year-old daughter of a man named Jairus.

Jairus lives with his wife and their only child near the Sea of Galilee. One day the young girl gets very sick, and Jairus can see that she is going to die. He begins to think about Jesus, that wonderful man Jairus has heard about who can heal people. So Jairus goes to look for him. He finds Jesus on the shore of the Sea of Galilee, teaching many people.

Jairus makes his way through the crowd and falls at Jesus' feet. He says to Jesus: 'My little daughter is very sick. Will you please come and help her? I beg you to come.' Right away, Jesus goes with Jairus. The crowd that has come to see the Great Teacher also follow along. But after they go a distance, some men come from the house of Jairus and tell him: "Your daughter died! Why bother the teacher any longer?"

What do we learn from Jesus' resurrection of Jairus' daughter?

Jesus overhears the men say this. He knows how sad Jairus is to lose his only child. So He tells him: 'Do not fear. Just have faith in God, and your daughter will be all right.' They keep on going until they come to Jairus' house. Here friends of the family are crying. They are sad because their little friend has died. But Jesus tells them: 'Stop weeping. The young child has not died, but she is sleeping.'

When Jesus says this, the people begin to laugh, for they know that the girl has died. Why, then, do you think Jesus says that she is sleeping?— What lesson do you think he wants to teach the people?— He wants them to know that death can be like a deep sleep. He wants to teach them that by means of God's power, he can bring a dead person back to life just as easily as we can wake a person up from sleep.

Jesus has everyone leave the house except his apostles Peter, James, and John and the girl's father and mother. Then he goes in where the young child is. He takes her by the hand and says: 'Young girl, get up!' And right away she gets up and begins walking! Her father and mother are just filled with joy.—Mark 5:21-24, 35-43; Luke 8:40-42, 49-56.

Now think about this. Since Jesus could bring that young girl back to life, can he do the same for others?— Do you think he will really do it?— Yes, he will. Jesus himself said: "The hour is coming in which all those in the memorial tombs will hear [my] voice and come out."—John 5:28, 29.

Do you think Jesus *wants* to resurrect people?— Another example in the Bible helps to answer that question. What happens one day near the city of Nain shows how Jesus feels about people who are grieving at funerals.

A woman is in the funeral procession for her son as the crowd leaves Nain. Earlier her husband died, and now her *only* child is dead. How sad she is! Many of the people of Nain are following along as her son's body is carried outside the city. The woman is weeping, and the people can do nothing to comfort her.

On this day, Jesus and his disciples happen to be coming toward the city of Nain. Near the city gate, they meet the crowd going to bury the woman's son. When Jesus sees the weeping woman, he is moved with pity for her. His heart is touched by her great sadness. He wants to help her.

So with tenderness and yet with firmness that makes her listen, he says: "Stop weeping." His manner and action cause everyone to watch him with interest. As Jesus goes over to the body, all must wonder what he is going to do. Jesus speaks, commanding: "Young man, I say to you, Get up!" Right away, he sits up! And he starts to speak.—Luke 7:11-17.

Imagine how the woman must have felt! How would you feel to receive a dead loved one back again?— Doesn't this show that Jesus truly loves people and *wants* to help them?— Just think how wonderful it will be in God's new world to welcome people back to life!—2 Peter 3:13; Revelation 21:3, 4.

At that time some of those resurrected will be people we knew before, including children. We will know who they are just as Jairus knew his daughter when Jesus resurrected her. Others will be people who died hundreds or thousands of years ago. But God will not forget them just because they lived long ago.

Isn't it wonderful to know that Jehovah God and his Son, Jesus, love us that much?— They want us to live, not for just a few years, but forever!

Concerning the Bible's wonderful hope for the dead, please read Isaiah 25:8; Acts 24:15; and 1 Corinthians 15:20-22.

What does the resurrection of this woman's only child show?

CHAPTER 36

WHO WILL BE RESURRECTED? WHERE WILL THEY LIVE?

IN THE last two chapters, how many people did we read about who were resurrected?— There were five. How many were children?— Three. And a fourth one is called a young man. What do you think this shows?—

Well, it shows that God loves young people. But he will resurrect many others too. Will God resurrect only those who did what is good?— We might think so. Yet, many people never learned the truth about Jehovah God and his Son. So they did what was bad because they were taught wrong things. Do you think that Jehovah will resurrect people like that?—

The Bible says: "There is going to be a resurrection of both the righteous and the unrighteous." (Acts 24:15) Why will those who were *not* righteous, or who did *not* do what was right, be resurrected?— It is because they never had a chance to learn about Jehovah and what he wants people to do.

Why will God resurrect some who did not do what was right?

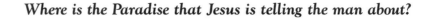

When do you think people will be resurrected?— Think back to when Lazarus died and Jesus promised his sister Martha: "Your brother will rise." Martha replied: "I know he will rise in the resurrection on the last day." (John 11:23, 24) What did Martha mean when she said that Lazarus would rise on "the last day"?—

Well, Martha had heard about Jesus' promise: 'All those in the memorial tombs will come out.' (John 5:28, 29) So "the last day" is when all those in God's memory will be brought back to life. This last day is not a 24-hour day. It will be a thousand years long. On this day, the Bible says, 'God will judge the people of the earth.' The ones he judges will include those who have been resurrected. —Acts 17:31; 2 Peter 3:8.

Think about what a wonderful day this will be! During this thousand-year-long day, many millions of people who have died will be brought back to life. Jesus calls the place where they are brought back to live Paradise. Let's see where Paradise will be and what it will be like there.

About three hours before Jesus dies on a torture stake, he talks about Paradise to a man on a stake next to him. The man is being put to death for crimes he has committed. But as this criminal watches Jesus and hears what is said about Him, he begins to believe in Jesus. So the criminal says: "Remember me when you get into your kingdom." Jesus answers: "Truly I tell you today, You will be with me in Paradise."—Luke 23:42, 43.

What does Jesus mean when he says this? Where is Paradise?— Think about it. Where was Paradise to begin with?— Remember, God gave the first man, Adam, and

When we read about Paradise, what should we picture in our minds?

his wife a paradise to live in right here on this earth. It was called the garden of Eden. There were animals in that garden, but they didn't hurt anyone. And there were trees with lots of delicious fruit on them, as well as a big river. It was a wonderful place to live!—Genesis 2:8-10.

So when we read of that criminal being in Paradise, we should picture in our minds this earth made into a beautiful place to live. Will Jesus be right here on earth with the former criminal in Paradise?— No. Do you know why he won't be here?—

It is because Jesus will be in heaven ruling as King over the Paradise on earth. So Jesus will be with that man in the sense that Jesus will raise him from the dead and care for his needs. But why will Jesus let a former criminal live in Paradise?— Let's see if we can figure that out.

Before the criminal talked to Jesus, did he know about God's purposes?— No, he didn't. He did bad things because he didn't know the truth about God. In Paradise he will be taught about God's purposes. Then he will have the opportunity to prove that he really does love God by doing His will.

Where will the resurrected ones live, and what will they do?

Will everyone who is resurrected live in Paradise on earth?— No, they won't. Do you know why not?— Because some will be resurrected to live with Jesus in heaven. They will rule with him as kings over the Paradise earth. Let's see how we know this.

The night before Jesus dies, he tells his apostles: 'In the house of my Father in heaven, there are many places to live, and I am going my way to prepare a place for you.' Then Jesus promises them: "I am coming again and will receive you home to myself, that where I am you also may be."—John 14:2, 3.

Where does Jesus go after he is resurrected?— Yes, back to heaven to be with his Father. (John 17:4, 5) So Jesus promises his apostles and other followers that he will resurrect them so that they can be with him in heaven. What will they do there with Jesus?— The Bible says that his disciples who have a part in "the first resurrection" will live in heaven and rule over the earth "as kings with him for the thousand years."—Revelation 5:10; 20:6; 2 Timothy 2:12.

How many will share in "the first resurrection" and rule with Jesus as kings?— Jesus told his disciples: "Have no fear, *little flock,* because your Father has approved of giving you the kingdom." (Luke 12:32) This "little flock," who are resurrected to be with Jesus in his heavenly Kingdom, are an exact number. The Bible shows that "a hundred and forty-four thousand" are resurrected from the earth.—Revelation 14:1, 3.

How many will live in Paradise on earth?— The Bible does not say. But God had told Adam and Eve while they were in the garden of Eden to have children and *fill the earth.* True, they failed to do that. But God will see to it that his purpose to have the earth filled with good people is carried out.—Genesis 1:28; Isaiah 45:18; 55:11.

Just think how wonderful it will be to live in Paradise! The whole earth will become like a park. It will be alive with birds and animals and beautiful with trees and flowers of every kind. No one will have pain because he is sick, nor will anyone have to die. Everyone will be a friend of everyone else. If we want to live forever in Paradise, now is the time to prepare for it.

Read more about God's purpose for the earth, at Proverbs 2:21, 22; Ecclesiastes 1:4; Isaiah 2:4; 11:6-9; 35:5, 6; and 65:21-24.

CHAPTER 37

REMEMBERING JEHOVAH AND HIS SON

SUPPOSE someone gave you a wonderful gift. How would you feel about it?— Would you just say thank you and then forget all about the one who gave it to you? Or would you remember him and what he did for you?—

Jehovah God gave us a wonderful gift. He sent his Son to earth to die for us. Do you know why Jesus had to die for us?— This is something very important that we should understand.

As we learned in Chapter 23, Adam sinned when he broke God's perfect law. And we received sin from Adam, the father of us all. So, what do you think we need?— We need, as it were, a new father, one who lived a perfect life on earth. Who do you think can be that father to us?— Jesus can.

Jehovah sent Jesus to earth so that he could become like a father to us instead of Adam. The Bible says: "'The first man Adam became a living soul.' The last Adam became a life-giving spirit." Who was the first Adam?— Yes, the one whom God created from the dust of the earth. Who is the second Adam?— Jesus. The Bible shows this when it says: "The first man [Adam] is out of the earth and made of dust; the second man [Jesus] *is out of heaven.*"—1 Corinthians 15:45, 47; Genesis 2:7.

Since God took Jesus' life from heaven and put it inside the woman Mary, Jesus did not get any sin from Adam. That is why

Jesus was a perfect man. (Luke 1:30-35) That is also why an angel said to the shepherds when Jesus was born: "There was born to you today a Savior." (Luke 2:11) But to be our Savior, what did the baby Jesus first need to do?— He needed to grow up and become a full-grown man, just like Adam. Then Jesus could become 'the second Adam.'

Jesus, our Savior, will also become our "Eternal Father." He is called that in the Bible. (Isaiah 9:6, 7) Yes, the *perfect* Jesus can become our father instead of Adam, who became imperfect when he sinned. That way we can choose to have 'the second Adam' as our father. Of course, Jesus himself is a Son of Jehovah God.

By coming to know about Jesus, we can receive him as our Savior. Do you remember what we need to be saved from?— Yes, from the sin and death that we inherited from Adam. The perfect life as a full-grown man that Jesus sacrificed, or gave up, for us is called the *ransom*. Jehovah provided the ransom so that we can have our sins taken away. —Matthew 20:28; Romans 5:8; 6:23.

Surely we don't want to forget what God and his Son have done for us, do we?— Jesus showed his followers a special way that can help

How were Adam and Jesus alike, and why was it so important that they were?

How did the lamb's blood protect the people of Israel?

us remember what he did. Let's talk about it.

Just imagine that you are in the upstairs room of a house in Jerusalem. It is nighttime. Jesus and his apostles are at a table. On the table, there are some roast lamb, flat loaves of bread, and red wine. They are having a special meal. Do you know why?—

This meal is to remind them of what Jehovah did hundreds of years earlier when his people, the Israelites, were slaves in Egypt. At that time Jehovah told his people: 'Kill a lamb for each family, and

What can Jesus' blood, which Jesus compared to wine, do for us?

put its blood on the doorposts of your houses.' Then he said: 'Go inside your houses, and eat the lamb.'

The Israelites did that. And that same night, God's angel passed through the land of Egypt. In most houses, the angel killed the firstborn child. But when the angel saw the lamb's blood on the doorposts, he passed over that house. In those houses, no children died. Pharaoh, the king of Egypt, was frightened by what Jehovah's angel had done. So Pharaoh told the Israelites: 'You are free to go. Get out of Egypt!' At that, they loaded up their camels and donkeys and left.

Jehovah did not want his people to forget how he set them free. So he said: 'Once a year you must eat a meal like the meal you ate tonight.' They called this special meal the Passover. Do you know why?— Because that night God's angel "passed over" the houses marked with blood.—Exodus 12:1-13, 24-27, 31.

Jesus and his apostles are thinking about this when they eat the Passover meal. Afterward, Jesus does something very important. Before he does, however, the unfaithful apostle, Judas, is dismissed. Then Jesus picks up one of the leftover loaves of bread, prays over it, breaks it, and passes it to his disciples. "Take, eat," he says. Then he tells them: 'This bread stands for my body that I will give when I die for you.'

Next Jesus picks up a cup of red wine. After another prayer of thanks, he passes it around and says: "Drink out of it, all of you." And he tells them: 'This wine stands for my blood. Soon I am going to pour out my blood to free you from your sins. Keep doing this to remember me.'—Matthew 26:26-28; 1 Corinthians 11:23-26.

Did you notice that Jesus said the disciples should keep doing this to remember him?— No longer would they have the Passover meal. Instead, once each year they would have this special meal to remember Jesus and his death. This meal is called the Lord's Evening Meal. Today we often call it the Memorial. Why?— Because it brings back to our memory what Jesus and his Father, Jehovah God, did for us.

The bread should make us think of Jesus' body. He was willing to give up that body so that we could have everlasting life. And what about the red wine?— That should remind us of the value of Jesus' blood. It is more precious than the blood of the Passover lamb in Egypt. Do you know why?— The Bible says that Jesus' blood can bring us forgiveness of sins. And when all our sins are taken away, we will no longer get sick, grow old, and die. We should think of that when we attend the Memorial.

Should everyone eat the bread and drink the wine at the Memorial?— Well, Jesus told those who do eat and drink: 'You will have part in my kingdom and sit on thrones in heaven with me.' (Luke 22:19, 20, 30) This meant that they would go to heaven to be kings with Jesus. So only those who have the hope of ruling with Jesus in heaven should take the bread and wine.

But even those who do not eat the bread or drink the wine should attend the Memorial. Do you know why?— Because Jesus gave his life for us too. By going to the Memorial, we show that we have not forgotten. We remember God's wonderful gift.

Scriptures that show the importance of Jesus' ransom include 1 Corinthians 5:7; Ephesians 1:7; 1 Timothy 2:5, 6; and 1 Peter 1:18, 19.

CHAPTER 38

WHY WE SHOULD LOVE JESUS

IMAGINE that you are in a boat that is sinking. Would you want someone to save you?— What if someone gave up his own life to do so?— Well, that is what Jesus Christ did. As we learned in Chapter 37, he gave his life as a ransom so that we could be saved.

Of course, Jesus does not save us from drowning. What does he save us from? Do you remember?— From the sin and death we all got from Adam. Even though some people have done very bad things, Jesus died for them too. Would you risk your life to try to save people like that?—

The Bible says: "Hardly will anyone die for a righteous man; indeed, for the good man, perhaps, someone even dares to die." Yet, the Bible explains that Jesus "died for ungodly men." That includes people who do not even serve God! The Bible says further: "While we were yet sinners [still doing bad things], Christ died for us."—Romans 5:6-8.

Can you think of an apostle who had once done very bad things?— That apostle wrote: "Christ Jesus came into the world to save sinners. *Of these I am foremost.*" The apostle who said that was Paul. He said that he was "once senseless" and that he had carried on "in badness."—1 Timothy 1:15; Titus 3:3.

Just think of how much love God had to send his Son to die for people like that! Why not get your Bible and read about this in John chapter 3, verse 16. There it says: "God loved the world [that is, the people who live on earth] so much that he gave his only-begotten Son, in order that everyone exercising faith in him might not be destroyed but have everlasting life."

Jesus proved that he had the same love for us that his Father had. You may remember that in Chapter 30 of this book, we read about some things Jesus suffered the night he was arrested. He was taken to the home of High Priest Caiaphas, where He was put on trial. False witnesses were brought in who told lies about Jesus, and the people hit him with their fists. That was when Peter denied knowing Jesus. Now let's pretend we are right there and can see what else happens.

Morning comes. Jesus has been up all night. Because the night trial was not a proper one, the priests quickly call together the Sanhedrin, or Jewish high court, and hold another trial. Here they again accuse Jesus of crimes against God.

The priests next have Jesus bound, and they lead him to Pilate, the Roman governor. They tell Pilate: 'Jesus is against the government. He should be killed.' But Pilate can see that the priests are telling lies. So Pilate tells them: 'I find nothing wrong with this man. I will let him go.' But the priests and others shout: 'No! Kill him!'

Later, Pilate again tries to tell the people that he is going to let Jesus go free. But the priests get the crowds to shout: 'If you let him go, you are against the government too! Kill him!' The crowds become very noisy. Do you know what Pilate does?—

He gives in. First he has Jesus whipped. Then he turns him over to soldiers to be put to death. They put a crown of thorns on Jesus' head and make fun of him by bowing down

before him. Then they give Jesus a big post, or stake, to carry and lead him outside the city to a spot called Skull Place. There they nail Jesus' hands and feet to the stake. Then they stand it up so that Jesus is hanging on it. He is bleeding. The pain is very great.

Jesus does not die right away. He just hangs there on the stake. The chief priests make fun of him. And passersby say: "If you are a son of God, come down off the torture stake!" But Jesus knows what his Father has sent him to do. He knows that he must give his perfect life so that we can have the chance to get everlasting life. Finally, about three o'clock that

What things did Jesus suffer when he gave his life for us?

*What can we do
to show that we love Jesus?*

afternoon, Jesus cries out to his Father and dies.—Matthew 26:36–27:50; Mark 15:1; Luke 22:39–23:46; John 18:1–19:30.

How different Jesus was from Adam! Adam did not show love for God. He disobeyed God. Neither did Adam show love for us. Because he sinned, all of us have been born in sin. But Jesus showed love for God and for us. He always obeyed God. And he gave his life so that he could take away the harm that Adam did to us.

Do you appreciate what a wonderful thing Jesus did?— When you pray to God, do you thank him for giving us his Son?— The apostle Paul appreciated what Christ did for him. Paul wrote that the Son of God *"loved me and handed himself over for me."* (Galatians 2:20) Jesus died for you and for me too. He gave his perfect life so that we can have everlasting life! Surely that is a strong reason why we should love Jesus.

The apostle Paul wrote to Christians in the city of Corinth: "The love of Christ puts us into action." Into what kind of action should Christ's love put us? What do you think?— Notice Paul's answer: "Christ died for everyone so that *they would live for Him. They should not live to please themselves."*—Italics ours; 2 Corinthians 5:14, 15, *New Life Version.*

Can you think of ways you can show that you are living to please Christ?— Well, one way is by telling others what you have learned about him. Or think about this: You may be alone, so your mother or father cannot see what you are doing, nor can any other human see you. Will you watch TV programs or perhaps look at things on the Internet that you know would not please Jesus?— Remember, Jesus is now alive, and he can see everything we do!

Another reason why we should love Jesus is that we want to copy Jehovah. "The Father loves me," Jesus said. Do you know why he loves Jesus and why we should too?— Because Jesus was willing to die so that God's will could be done. (John 10: 17) So let's do what the Bible tells us: "Become imitators of God, as beloved children, and go on walking in love, just as the Christ also loved you and delivered himself up for you." —Ephesians 5:1, 2.

To build appreciation for Jesus and for what he did for us, please read John 3:35; 15:9, 10; and 1 John 5:11, 12.

Who can see everything we do?

CHAPTER 39

GOD REMEMBERS HIS SON

JESUS cried when his friend Lazarus died. Do you think that Jehovah felt bad when Jesus suffered and died?— The Bible says that God can "feel hurt" and even be "pained" by things that happen.—Psalm 78:40, 41; John 11:35.

Can you imagine the pain Jehovah felt as he watched his dear Son die?— Jesus was sure that God would not forget him. That is why his last words before he died were: "Father, into your hands I entrust my [life]."—Luke 23:46.

Jesus was sure that he would be resurrected, that he would not be left "in hell," or the grave. After Jesus was raised up, the apostle Peter quoted what was written in the Bible about Jesus, saying: "His soul was not left in hell, neither his flesh did see corruption." (Acts 2:31, *King James Version*; Psalm 16:10) No, the body of Jesus never had time to become corrupt in the grave, that is, to decay and smell bad.

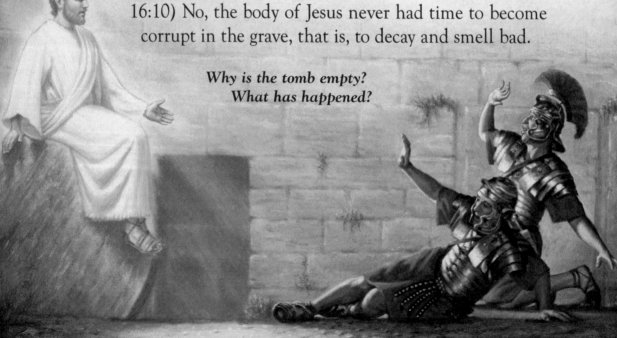

Why is the tomb empty?
What has happened?

When Jesus was on earth, he even told his disciples that he would not be dead very long. He explained to them that he would "be killed, and *on the third day* be raised up." (Luke 9:22) So, really, the disciples should not have been surprised when Jesus was resurrected. But were they?— Let's see.

It is about three o'clock Friday afternoon when the Great Teacher dies on the torture stake. Joseph, a rich member of the Sanhedrin, is also a secret believer in Jesus. When he learns that Jesus is dead, he goes to Pilate, the Roman governor. He asks if he can take Jesus' body down from the stake to bury it. Afterward, Joseph carries Jesus' body to a garden where there is a tomb, which is a place where dead bodies are put.

After the body is put in the tomb, a big stone is rolled in front. So the tomb is closed. Now it is *the third day,* which is Sunday. It is before sunrise, so it is still dark. Men are there guarding the tomb. The chief priests sent them to do it. Do you know why?—

The priests too had heard that Jesus said he would be resurrected. So to keep his disciples from stealing the body and then saying that Jesus was raised up, the priests have guards posted. Suddenly, the ground begins to shake. In the darkness, there is a flash of light. It is an angel of Jehovah! The soldiers are so frightened that they cannot move. The angel goes to the tomb and rolls the stone away. The tomb is empty!

Yes, it is as the apostle Peter later said: "This Jesus God resurrected." (Acts 2:32) God made Jesus alive with a body like the one Jesus had before he came to earth. He was resurrected with a spirit body like the angels have. (1 Peter 3:18) So if people are to see Jesus, he must make himself a body of flesh. Is that what he does?— Let's see.

Now the sun is coming up. The soldiers have gone away. Mary Magdalene and other women disciples of Jesus are on their way to the tomb. They are saying among themselves: 'Who will roll that heavy stone away for us?' (Mark 16:3) But when they get to the tomb, the stone has already been rolled away. And the tomb is empty! Jesus' dead body of flesh is gone! Right away, Mary Magdalene runs off to find some of Jesus' apostles.

The other women stay by the tomb. They wonder: 'Where could Jesus' body be?' Suddenly two men in flashing clothing appear. They are angels! They say to the women: 'Why are you looking for Jesus here? He was raised up. Go quickly and tell his disciples.' Well, you can imagine how fast the women run! On the way, a man meets them. Do you know who he is?—

It is Jesus, who has taken on a fleshly body! He also says to the women: 'Go and tell my disciples.' The women are excited. They find the disciples and tell them: 'Jesus is alive! We saw him!' Mary has already told Peter and John about the empty tomb. Now they visit it, as you can see here. They look at the linen cloths Jesus was wrapped in, but they aren't sure what to think. They want to believe that Jesus is alive again, but it seems too wonderful to be true.

Later that Sunday, Jesus appears to two of his disciples who are walking along the road to the village of Emmaus. Jesus walks and talks with them, but they don't recognize him because he doesn't have the same fleshly body that he had before. It is not until Jesus has a meal with them and says a prayer that they recognize him. The disciples are so excited that they hurry many miles back to Jerusalem! Perhaps it is shortly after this that Jesus makes an appearance to Peter to show him that He is alive.

Then later that Sunday evening, many disciples are gathered in a room. The doors are locked. Suddenly, Jesus is right there in the room with them! Now they know that the Great Teacher really is alive again. Imagine how happy they are!—Matthew 28:1-15; Luke 24:1-49; John 19:38–20:21.

For 40 days Jesus appears in different bodies of flesh to show his disciples that he is alive. Then he leaves the earth and goes

What may Peter and John be thinking?

back to his Father in heaven. (Acts 1:9-11) Soon the disciples start telling everyone that God raised Jesus up from the dead. Even when the priests beat them and have some of them killed, they keep preaching. They know that if they die, God will remember them just as he remembered his Son.

How different those early followers of Jesus were from many people today! These people think only about Easter rabbits and colored Easter eggs at the time of year when Jesus was resurrected. But the Bible doesn't say anything about Easter rabbits and eggs. It talks about serving God.

At the time of year Jesus was resurrected, what do many think about? But what do you think about?

We can be like Jesus' disciples by telling people that God did a wonderful thing when he resurrected his Son. We never need to be afraid, even if people say they will kill us. If we should die, Jehovah will remember us and resurrect us, just as he did Jesus.

Aren't we glad to know that God remembers those who serve him and will even resurrect them from the dead?— Knowing these things should cause us to want to know how we can make God happy. Did you know that we really can?— Let's talk about this next.

Belief in Jesus' resurrection should make our hope firm and our faith strong. Please read Acts 2:22-36; 4:18-20; and 1 Corinthians 15:3-8, 20-23.

HOW TO MAKE GOD HAPPY

WHAT can we do to make God happy? Can we give him anything?— Jehovah says: "To me belongs every wild animal of the forest." He also says: "The silver is mine, and the gold is mine." (Psalm 24:1; 50:10; Haggai 2:8) Yet, there is something we can give to God. What is it?—

Jehovah allows us to choose whether we will serve him or not. He does not force us to do what he wants us to do. Let's try to figure out why God made us so that we can choose whether we will serve him or not.

You may know what a robot is. It is a machine that is made so that it will do whatever its maker wants it to do. So the robot has no choice. Jehovah could have made us all to be like robots. He could have made us so that we could do only what he wanted us to do. But God didn't do that. Do you know why?— Well, some toys are robots. When a button is pressed, they do just what the maker of the toy designed them to do. Have you ever seen a toy like that?— Often people get tired of playing with a toy that does only what it has been made, or programmed, to do. God doesn't want us to obey him because we are robots

Why didn't God make us to be like this robot?

that are programmed to serve him. Jehovah wants us to serve him because we *love* him and because we *want* to obey him.

How do you think our heavenly Father feels when we obey him because we want to?— Well, tell me, how does the way you behave affect your parents?— The Bible says that a wise son "makes [his] father rejoice" but that a foolish son "is the grief of his mother." (Proverbs 10:1) Have you noticed that when you do what your mother and father ask you to do, it makes them happy?— But how do they feel when you disobey them?—

How can you make both Jehovah and your parents happy?

Now let's think of our heavenly Father, Jehovah. He tells us how we can make him happy. Why not get your Bible and open it to Proverbs 27:11. There God is speaking to us: "Be wise, my son [or, we might also say, my daughter], and *make my heart rejoice*, that I may make a reply to him that is taunting me." Do you know what it means to taunt someone?— Well, a person may taunt you by laughing at you and saying that you are not able to do what you said you could do. How does Satan taunt Jehovah?— Let's see.

Remember, we learned in Chapter 8 of this book that Satan wants to be Number One and that he wants everyone to obey him. Satan says that people worship Jehovah only because Jehovah will give them everlasting life if they do. After Satan got Adam and Eve to disobey Jehovah, Satan challenged God. He told God: 'People serve you only for what they get from you. Just give me the chance, and I can turn anybody away from you.'

Now it's true, those exact words are not found in the Bible. But when we read about the man Job, it becomes clear that Satan said something like that to God. It really did matter, both to Satan and to Jehovah, whether Job was faithful to God or not. Let's open our Bibles to Job chapters 1 and 2 to see what happened.

Notice in Job chapter 1 that Satan is right there in heaven when the angels come to see Jehovah. So Jehovah asks Satan: "Where do you come from?" Satan answers that he has been looking around the earth. So Jehovah asks: 'Have

After Adam and Eve sinned, how did Satan challenge Jehovah?

you noticed Job, that he serves me and does nothing bad?'—Job 1:6-8.

Right away Satan makes excuses. 'Job only worships you because he doesn't have any troubles. If you take your protection and blessing away from him, he will curse you to your face.' So Jehovah answers: 'All right, Satan, you can do anything you want to him, but don't hurt Job himself.'—Job 1:9-12.

What does Satan do?— He has people steal Job's cattle and donkeys and kill those taking care of them. Then lightning strikes, destroying the sheep and their caretakers. Later, people come and steal the camels and kill those looking after them. Finally, Satan causes a windstorm that knocks down the house where Job's ten children are, and all of them are killed. Despite all of this, Job still serves Jehovah.—Job 1:13-22.

When Jehovah sees Satan again, Jehovah points out that Job is still faithful. Satan makes excuses, saying: 'If you just let me hurt his body, he will curse you to your face.' So Jehovah lets Satan hurt Job's body but warns him not to kill Job.

What did Job endure,
and why did this make God happy?

Satan strikes Job so that his whole body breaks out with sores. These smell so bad that nobody wants to be near him. Even Job's wife tells him: "Curse God and die!" Those who pretend to be Job's friends come to visit and make him feel worse by saying that he must have done terrible things to have all this trouble. Despite all the trouble and pain Satan causes Job, however, Job keeps on serving Jehovah faithfully.—Job 2:1-13; 7:5; 19:13-20.

How do you think Job's faithfulness made Jehovah feel?— It made him happy because Jehovah could tell Satan: 'Look at Job! He serves me because he *wants* to.' Will you be like Job, a person Jehovah can point to as an example that proves Satan a liar?— Really, it is a privilege to provide an answer to Satan's claim that he can turn anyone away from serving Jehovah. Jesus certainly considered it a privilege.

The Great Teacher never allowed Satan to get Him to do anything wrong. Just think how his example made his Father happy! Jehovah could point to Jesus and reply to Satan: 'Look at my Son! He has kept perfect faithfulness to me because he loves me!' Think, too, what joy Jesus has in making his Father's heart glad. Because of that joy, Jesus even endured death on a torture stake.—Hebrews 12:2.

Do you want to be like our Great Teacher and make Jehovah happy?— Then keep on learning about what Jehovah wants you to do, and make him happy by doing it!

Read what Jesus did to make God happy and what we need to do as well, at Proverbs 23:22-25; John 5:30; 6:38; 8:28; and 2 John 4.

CHAPTER 41

CHILDREN WHO
MAKE GOD HAPPY

WHAT child on earth do you think made Jehovah the happiest?— It was his Son, Jesus. Let's talk about things Jesus did to make his heavenly Father happy.

Jesus' family lived about a three-day journey from Jerusalem, where the beautiful temple of Jehovah was located. Jesus called the temple "the house of my Father." He and his family went there every year to attend the Passover.

One year, when Jesus was 12, his family began the return trip after the Passover. It was not until they stopped for the night that they noticed that Jesus was nowhere to be found among their relatives and friends. So right away Mary and Joseph went back to Jerusalem to find Jesus. Where do you suppose he was?—

They found Jesus in the temple. He was listening to the teachers, and he was asking them questions. And when they asked him something, he would answer. They were amazed at the fine answers he gave. Can you see why God was happy with his Son?—

Of course, when Mary and Joseph finally found Jesus, they felt much better. But Jesus had not been worried. He knew that the temple was a good place to be. So he asked: "Did you not know that I must be in the house of my Father?" He knew that the temple was God's house, and he loved to be there.

Afterward, Mary and Joseph took 12-year-old Jesus back home with them to Nazareth. How do you think Jesus treated his parents?— Well, the Bible says that he "*continued subject to them.*" What do you think that means?— It means that he was *obedient* to them. Yes, he did what his parents asked him to do, even if this was something like bringing water from the well.—Luke 2:41-52.

So think about this: *Even though Jesus was perfect, he obeyed his imperfect parents.* Did this make God happy?— It certainly did, for God's Word tells children: "Be obedient to your parents." (Ephesians 6:1) You too will make God happy if you obey your parents, as Jesus did.

Another way you can make God happy is by telling others about him. Now some people may say that this is not what young people should be doing. But when people tried to stop young boys from doing this, Jesus said: 'Did you never read in the

How did the child Jesus make God happy?

Scriptures, "Out of the mouths of little children God will bring forth praise"?' (Matthew 21:16) So we can all tell others about Jehovah and about what a wonderful God he is, if we really want to. And if we do, we will make God happy.

Where do we learn things about God that we can talk to others about?— From our Bible study at home. But we learn more at the place where God's people meet to study. But how can we tell who are his people?—

Well, what do the people do at their meetings? Do they really teach what is in the Bible? Do they read it and discuss it? That is how we listen to God, isn't it?— And at Christian meetings we would expect to hear what God says, wouldn't we?— But what if people say that you do not have to live the way the Bible says? Would you say that they are God's people?—

Here is something else to think about. The Bible says that God's people would be "a people for his name." (Acts 15:14) Since God's name is Jehovah, we can ask people if Jehovah is their God. If they say no, then we know that they are not his people. God's people would also be talking to others about God's Kingdom. And they would show their love for God by keeping his commandments.—1 John 5:3.

If you know people who do all those things, then you should meet with them for worship. You should listen carefully at these meetings and then give answers when questions are asked. That is what Jesus did when he was in God's house. And if you do those things, you will make God happy, just as Jesus did.

Can you think of other children mentioned in the Bible who made God happy?— Timothy is an outstanding exam-

214

*Although his father was not a believer,
what did Timothy want to do?*

ple. His father was not a believer in Jehovah. But his mother, Eunice, was, and so was his grandmother Lois. Timothy listened to them and learned about Jehovah.

When Timothy had grown older, the apostle Paul visited the town where he lived. He noticed how much Timothy wanted to serve Jehovah. So he invited Timothy to come with him to serve God in an even bigger way. Everywhere they traveled, they told people about the Kingdom of God and about Jesus.—Acts 16: 1-5; 2 Timothy 1:5; 3:14, 15.

But are the examples in the Bible of only young boys who made God happy?— Not at all. Consider a young Israelite girl who did. When she was living, the nation of Syria and the nation of Israel were enemies. One day the Syrians fought against Israel and took that young girl captive. She was sent to the house of the army chief, who was called Naaman.

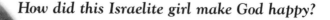

How did this Israelite girl make God happy?

There she came to be the servant of Naaman's wife.

Now Naaman had a sickness called leprosy. None of the doctors had been able to help him. But the young girl from Israel believed that one of God's special servants, a prophet, could help Naaman. Of course, Naaman and his wife did not worship Jehovah. Should the young girl tell them what she knew? What would you have done?—

Well, the little girl said: 'If only Naaman would go to Jehovah's prophet in Israel, in that case, Naaman would be healed from his leprosy.' Naaman listened to the girl, and he went to Jehovah's prophet. When he did what the prophet told him to do, he was healed. This caused Naaman to become a worshiper of the true God.—2 Kings 5:1-15.

Would you like to help someone to learn about Jehovah and about what he can do, as that young girl did?— Who is there that you could help?— Of course, at first they might not think that they need help. But you could talk to them about the good things that Jehovah does. And they might listen. You can be sure that this will make God happy.

Further encouragement for young folks to take pleasure in serving God can be found at Psalm 122:1 (121:1, "Dy"); 148:12, 13; Ecclesiastes 12:1; 1 Timothy 4:12; and Hebrews 10:23-25.

CHAPTER 42

WHY WE NEED TO WORK

WHAT do you like best, to work or to play?— Really, there is nothing wrong with playing. The Bible speaks of Jerusalem being "filled with boys and girls playing in her public squares."—Zechariah 8:5.

The Great Teacher enjoyed watching children at play. Before he came to earth, he said: "I came to be beside [God] as a master worker . . . being glad before him all the time." Notice that Jesus was a worker with Jehovah in heaven. And when he was there, he said: "The things I was fond of were with the sons of men." Yes, as we have learned before, the Great Teacher had a real interest in everyone, including young ones.
—Proverbs 8:30, 31.

What did the Great Teacher enjoy before he came to earth?

Do you think Jesus played when he was a child?— He probably did. But since he had been "a master worker" in heaven, did he also work on earth?— Well, Jesus was called "the carpenter's son." But he was also called "the carpenter." What does this show?— Joseph, who raised Jesus as his son, must have taught him. So Jesus also became a carpenter.—Matthew 13:55; Mark 6:3.

What kind of carpenter was Jesus?— Since he was a master worker in heaven, don't you think he became a master carpenter on earth?— Consider what hard work it was to be a carpenter at that time. Jesus probably had to go out and cut down

What two kinds of work did Jesus do when he was on earth?

a tree, cut the tree into pieces, carry the wood home, and then shape the wood to make it into tables, benches, and other things.

Do you think this work brought Jesus pleasure?— Would you be happy if you could make fine tables and chairs and other things for people to use?— The Bible says it is good for one to "rejoice in his works." Work gives a kind of pleasure that you cannot get from play.—Ecclesiastes 3:22.

Really, work is good for both our minds and our bodies. Many children just sit and watch TV or play video games. They become overweight and weak, and they're really not happy. And they don't make others happy either. What do we need to do to be happy?—

We learned in Chapter 17 of this book that giving and doing things to help others bring happiness. (Acts 20:35) The Bible calls Jehovah "the happy God." (1 Timothy 1:11) And, as we read in Proverbs, Jesus was "glad before him all the time." Why was Jesus happy?— Well, he gave one of the reasons when he said: "My Father has kept working until now, and I keep working."—John 5:17.

When Jesus was on earth, he did not work as a carpenter all his life. Jehovah God had special work for him to do on earth. Do you know what it was?— Jesus said: "I must declare the good news of the kingdom of God, because for this I was sent forth." (Luke 4:43) Sometimes when Jesus preached to people, they believed him and told others the things he had said, as the Samaritan woman you see here did.—John 4:7-15, 27-30.

How did Jesus feel about doing this work? Do you think that he wanted to do it?— Jesus said: "My food is for me to do the will of him that sent me and to finish his work." (John 4:34) How much do you like to eat your favorite food?— This gives you an idea of how much Jesus liked the work that God gave him to do.

God made us so that learning to work helps to make us happy. He says that His gift to man is that he should "rejoice in his hard work." So if you learn to work when you are young, your whole life will be more enjoyable.—Ecclesiastes 5:19.

That does not mean that a young child can do the work of an older person, but we can all do some work. Your parents may go out to work day after day to earn money so that your family has food to eat and a home to live in. And as you should know, there is much work that needs to be done around the home to keep it neat and clean.

What work is there that you can do that will be a blessing to the whole family?— You can help set the table, wash the dishes, take out the garbage, clean your room, and pick up your toys. Perhaps you already do some of those things. That work really is a blessing to the family.

Let's see how work like that is a blessing. Toys are to be put away after you play. Why would you say that this is important?— It helps to keep the house neat, and it can also prevent accidents. If you don't pick up your toys, your mother may come along someday with her arms full and step on one of them. She may trip and fall and hurt herself. She may even have to go to the hospital. Wouldn't that be terrible?— So when you put away your toys after you play, that is a blessing to all.

There is other work that children have too. For example,

schoolwork. At school you learn how to read. Some children find reading to be fun, but others say it is hard. Even if it seems hard at first, you will be glad if you learn to read well. When you know how to read, there are many interesting things that you can learn. You will even be able to read for yourself God's own book, the Bible. So when you do your schoolwork well, it is really a blessing, isn't it?—

There are some people who try to avoid work. Maybe you know someone who does that. But since God made us to work, we need to learn how to enjoy it. How much did the Great Teacher enjoy his work?— It was like eating his favorite food. And what work was he talking about?— Telling others about Jehovah God and how they can receive everlasting life.

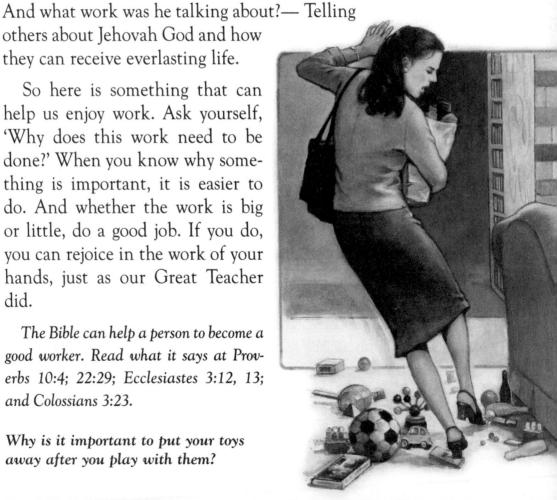

So here is something that can help us enjoy work. Ask yourself, 'Why does this work need to be done?' When you know why something is important, it is easier to do. And whether the work is big or little, do a good job. If you do, you can rejoice in the work of your hands, just as our Great Teacher did.

The Bible can help a person to become a good worker. Read what it says at Proverbs 10:4; 22:29; Ecclesiastes 3:12, 13; and Colossians 3:23.

Why is it important to put your toys away after you play with them?

CHAPTER 43

WHO ARE OUR BROTHERS AND SISTERS?

ONCE the Great Teacher asked a surprising question. It was: "Who is my mother, and who are my brothers?" (Matthew 12:48) Could you answer that question?— You probably know that the mother of Jesus was named Mary. But do you know the names of his brothers?— Did he have sisters too?—

The Bible says that Jesus' brothers were named "James and Joseph and Simon and Judas." And Jesus had sisters who were alive when he was preaching. Since Jesus was the firstborn, these were all younger than he was.—Matthew 13:55, 56; Luke 1:34, 35.

Were Jesus' brothers also his disciples?— The Bible says that at first they were "not exercising faith in him." (John 7:5) Later, however, James and Judas (also called Jude) became his disciples, and they even wrote books of the Bible. Do you know which books they wrote?— Yes, James and Jude.

Although Jesus' sisters are not named in the Bible, we know that he had at least two. However, there could have been more. Did these sisters become his followers?— The Bible doesn't say, so we don't know. But do you know why Jesus asked the question, "Who is my mother, and who are my brothers?"— Let's find out.

Jesus had been teaching his disciples when someone interrupted him to say: "Your mother and your brothers are standing outside, seeking to speak to you." So Jesus used the opportunity to teach an important lesson by asking that surprising question: "Who is my mother, and who are my brothers?" He extended his hand toward his disciples and answered it, exclaiming: "Look! My mother and my brothers!"

Then Jesus explained what he meant, saying: "Whoever does the will of my Father who is in heaven, the same is my brother, and sister, and mother." (Matthew 12:47-50) This shows how close Jesus felt to his disciples. He was teaching us that his disciples were like real brothers, sisters, and mothers to him.

At that time Jesus' own brothers—James, Joseph, Simon, and Judas—did not believe that Jesus was God's Son. They must not have believed what the angel Gabriel had told their mother. (Luke 1:30-33) So they may have been mean to Jesus. Anyone who acts like that is not being a *real* brother or

Who did Jesus explain were his brothers and sisters?

sister. Do you know of anyone who has been mean to his brother or sister?—

The Bible tells about Esau and Jacob and how Esau became so angry that he said: "I am going to kill Jacob my brother." Their mother, Rebekah, was so afraid that she had Jacob sent away so that Esau could not kill him. (Genesis 27:41-46) However, many years later Esau changed, and he hugged and kissed Jacob.—Genesis 33:4.

In time, Jacob had 12 sons. But the older sons of Jacob didn't love their younger brother Joseph. They were jealous of him because he was the favorite son of their father. So they sold him to slave traders who were on their way to Egypt. Then they told their father that Joseph had been killed by a wild beast. (Genesis 37:23-36) Wasn't that terrible?—

Later Joseph's brothers were sorry for what they had done. So Joseph forgave them. Can you see how Joseph was like Jesus?— Jesus' own

What lesson should we learn from what Cain did to Abel?

apostles ran away when he was in trouble, and Peter even denied knowing him. Yet, like Joseph, Jesus forgave them all.

Then there are the two brothers Cain and Abel. We can learn a lesson from them too. God saw in Cain's heart that he did not really love his brother. So God told Cain that he should change his ways. If Cain had really loved God, he would have paid attention. But he did not love God. One day Cain said to Abel: "Let us go over into the field." Abel went along with Cain. While they were there in the field alone, Cain hit his brother so hard that he killed him.—Genesis 4:2-8.

The Bible tells us that there is a special lesson we should learn from that. Do you know what it is?— 'This is the message which you have heard from the beginning: We should have love for one another; not like Cain, who came from the wicked one.' So brothers and sisters should have love for one another. They should not be like Cain.—1 John 3:11, 12.

Why would it be bad to be like Cain?— Because the Bible says that he 'came from the wicked one,' Satan the Devil. Since Cain acted like the Devil, it was just as if the Devil was his father.

Do you see why it is important to love your brothers and sisters?— If you do not love them, whose children would you be imitating?— Children of the Devil. You wouldn't want to be that, would you?— So how can you prove that you want to be a child of God?— It is by really loving your brothers and sisters.

But what is love?— Love is a deep feeling inside us that makes us want to do good things for other people. We show that we love others when we have a good feeling toward them and when we do good things for them. And who are our brothers and sisters whom we should love?— Remember, Jesus taught that they are the ones who make up the big Christian family.

How important is it that we love these Christian brothers and sisters?— The Bible says: "He who does not love his brother [or his sister], whom he has seen, cannot be loving God, whom he has not seen." (1 John 4:20) So we cannot love just a few in the Christian family. We must love them all. Jesus said: "By this all will know that you are my disciples, if you have love among yourselves." (John 13:35) Do you love all the brothers and sisters?— Remember, if you don't, you cannot really be loving God.

How can we show that we really love our brothers and sisters?— Well, if we love them, we won't stay away from them because we don't want to talk to them. We will be friendly to all of them. We will always do good to them and be willing to share. And if ever they are in trouble, we will come to their aid because we are truly a big family.

How can you show that you love your brother?

When we really do love all our brothers and sisters, what does it prove?— It proves that we are disciples of Jesus, the Great Teacher. And isn't that what we want to be?—

Showing love for our brothers and sisters is also discussed at Galatians 6:10 and 1 John 4:8, 21. Why not open your own Bible and read those texts?

226

CHAPTER 44

OUR FRIENDS SHOULD LOVE GOD

FRIENDS are people we like to talk to and spend time with. But it is important to have the right kind of friends. Who do you think is the best friend we can have?— Yes, Jehovah God.

Can we really be friends of God?— Well, the Bible says that Abraham, a man who lived long ago, was "Jehovah's friend." (James 2:23) Do you know why he was?— The Bible answers that Abraham *obeyed* God. He obeyed even when what he was asked to do was hard. So to be Jehovah's friend, we must do what pleases him, just as Abraham did and just as the Great Teacher has always done.—Genesis 22:1-14; John 8:28, 29; Hebrews 11:8, 17-19.

Why was Abraham "Jehovah's friend"?

Why did Jesus often stay with this family on visits to Jerusalem?
Do you know their names?

Jesus told his apostles: "You are my friends *if you do what I am commanding you.*" (John 15:14) Since everything that Jesus told people came from Jehovah, Jesus was saying that his friends were people who did what God said they should do. Yes, all his friends loved God.

Some of the closest friends of the Great Teacher were his apostles, whose pictures you can see on page 75 of this book. They traveled with him and helped him do the preaching work. Jesus spent much of his time with these men. They ate together. They talked about God together. And they did other things together. But Jesus had many other friends. He would stay with them, and they had good times together.

One family that Jesus liked to stay with lived in the small town of Bethany, just outside the big city of Jerusalem. Do you remember them?— They were Mary and Martha and their brother, Lazarus. Jesus called Lazarus his friend. (John 11:1, 5, 11) The reason Jesus loved this family and enjoyed being with them was that they loved Jehovah and served Him.

This does not mean that Jesus was not kind to people who did not serve God. He was. He even went to their homes and ate with them. This caused some to say that Jesus was "a friend of tax collectors and sinners." (Matthew 11:19) The fact is that Jesus didn't go to the homes of these people because he liked the way they lived. He visited them so that he could talk to them about Jehovah. He tried to help them to change from their bad ways and to serve God.

This happened one day in the city of Jericho. Jesus was just passing through on his way to Jerusalem. There was a crowd of people, and in the crowd was a man named Zacchaeus. He wanted to get a look at Jesus. But Zacchaeus was short, and he could not see because of the crowd. So he ran ahead along the road and climbed a tree in order to get a good look when Jesus went by.

When Jesus came to that tree, he looked up and said: 'Hurry and get down, for today I will come to your

Why has Zacchaeus climbed this tree?

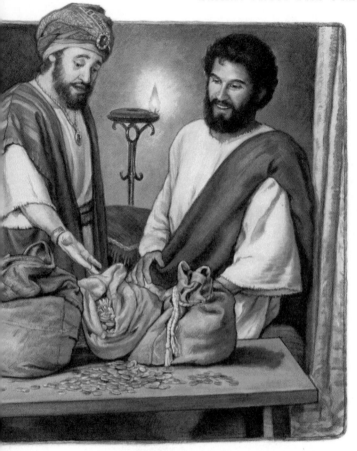

Why is Jesus visiting Zacchaeus, and what is Zacchaeus promising to do?

house.' But Zacchaeus was a rich man who had done bad things. Why did Jesus want to go to the house of such a man?—

It was not because Jesus liked the way that man lived. He went there to talk to Zacchaeus about God. He saw how that man had tried hard to see him. So he knew that Zacchaeus would probably listen. This was a good time to talk to him about the way that God says people should live.

So, what do we see happening now?— Zacchaeus likes the teachings of Jesus. He feels very sorry for having cheated people, and he is promising to give back money that he had no right to take. Then he becomes a follower of Jesus. Only then do Jesus and Zacchaeus become friends.—Luke 19:1-10.

If we learn from the Great Teacher, will we ever visit people who are not our friends?— Yes. But we won't go to their house because we like the way they live. And we won't do wrong things with them. We will visit them so that we can talk to them about God.

But our close friends are the ones we especially like to spend time with. To be the right kind of friends, they must be the kind that God likes. Some may not even know who Jehovah is. But if they want to learn about him, we can help them. And when the time comes that they love Jehovah as we do, then we can become close friends.

There is another way to find out if a person would make a good friend. Watch the things that he does. Does he do unkind things to other people and then laugh about it? That's not right, is it?— Is he always getting into trouble? We wouldn't want to get into trouble with him, would we?— Or does he do bad things on purpose and then think that he is smart because he didn't get caught? Even if that person didn't get caught, God saw what he did, didn't He?— Do you think that people who do such things would be good friends for us to have?—

Why not get your Bible? Let's see what it says about how our companions affect our lives. The scripture is at 1 Corinthians chapter 15, verse 33. Do you have it?— It reads: "Do not be misled. Bad associations spoil useful habits." This means that if we go with bad people, we may become bad. And it is also true that good companions help us to form good habits.

Let's never forget that the most important Person in our life is Jehovah. We don't want to spoil our friendship with him, do we?— So we must be careful to make friends with only those who love God.

The importance of the right kind of companions is shown at Psalm 119: 115 (118:115, "Dy"); Proverbs 13:20; 2 Timothy 2:22; and 1 John 2:15.

CHAPTER 45

WHAT IS GOD'S KINGDOM?
HOW TO SHOW WE WANT IT

D O YOU know the prayer Jesus taught his followers?—
If you don't, we can read it together from the Bible,
at Matthew 6:9-13. The prayer, which many call the
Lord's Prayer, includes the words: "Let your kingdom come."
Do you know what God's Kingdom is?—

Well, a king is the ruler of a country or territory. And his government is called a kingdom. In some countries the head person in the government is called the president. What is the Ruler of God's government called?— The King. That is why God's government is called the Kingdom.

Do you know whom Jehovah God picked to be King of His government?— His Son, Jesus Christ. Why is he better than any ruler that men may choose?— It is because Jesus really loves his Father, Jehovah. So he always does what is right.

What work did Jesus come to earth to do?

Long before Jesus was born in Bethlehem, the Bible told about his birth and said that he would become God's chosen Ruler. Let's read about this, at Isaiah 9:6, 7, from the *King James Version*. It says: "Unto us a child is born, unto us a son is given: and *the government* shall be upon his shoulder: and his name shall be called . . . *The Prince of Peace*. Of the increase of *his government* and peace there shall be no end."—Italics ours.

Do you know why the Ruler of God's Kingdom is here called "The Prince"?— Well, this prince is the son of a king. And Jesus is the Son of the Great King, Jehovah. But Jehovah has also made Jesus the King of His government, which will rule the earth for a thousand years. (Revelation 20:6) After Jesus was baptized, he began "preaching and saying: 'Repent, you people, for the kingdom of the heavens has drawn near.'"—Matthew 4:17.

Why, do you think, did Jesus say that the Kingdom had come near?— Because the King, who would later rule in heaven, was right there with them! That is why Jesus told people: "The kingdom of God is in your midst." (Luke 17:21) Wouldn't you like to have Jehovah's King so close to you that you could even touch him?—

So tell me, what important work did Jesus come to earth to do?— Jesus answered that question, saying: "Also to other cities *I must declare the good news of the kingdom of God*, because for this I was sent forth." (Luke 4:43) Jesus knew that he could not do all the preaching himself. So, what do you think he did?—

Jesus took people along with him and showed them how to do the preaching work. The first ones he trained were the 12 he chose as apostles. (Matthew 10:5, 7) But did Jesus train only his apostles to do this work? No, the Bible says that Jesus also trained many others to preach. In time, he sent out ahead of him 70 other disciples in groups of two. And what did they teach people?— Jesus said: "Go on telling them, 'The kingdom of God has come near to you.'" (Luke 10:9) In this way the people learned about God's government.

Long before in Israel, new kings would ride into the city on a colt to show themselves to the people. Now this is what Jesus does as he visits Jerusalem for the last time. You see, Jesus is going to be the Ruler of God's Kingdom. Do the people want him as King?—

Well, as he rides along, most of the crowd begin laying their outer garments on the road in front of him. Others cut down branches from the trees and put these on the road. By doing this they show that they want Jesus to be their King. They cry out: "Blessed is the One coming as the King in Jehovah's name!" But not everyone is happy. In fact, some religious leaders even say to Jesus, 'Tell your disciples to be quiet.'—Luke 19:28-40.

Five days later Jesus is arrested and is taken inside a palace to appear before the governor, Pontius Pilate. Jesus' enemies say that Jesus claims to be a king and that he is against the Roman government. So Pilate asks Jesus about this. Jesus shows that he is not trying to take over the government. He tells Pilate: "My kingdom is no part of this world."—John 18:36.

Pilate then goes outside and tells the people that he finds no fault with Jesus. But now the people don't want Jesus to be their King. They don't want him to be set free. (John 18:37-40) After talking with Jesus again, Pilate is sure that he has not done any-

thing wrong. So, finally, after bringing Jesus outside for the last time, Pilate says: "See! Your king!" But the people shout: "Take him away! Take him away! Impale him!"

Why do the people change their minds about wanting Jesus as King?

Pilate asks: "Shall I impale your king?" The chief priests answer: "We have no king but Caesar." Can you imagine that? Those wicked priests have been able to turn the people against Jesus!—John 19:1-16.

Today it is very much as it was then. Most people really don't want Jesus to be their King. They may say that they believe in God, but they don't want God or Christ to tell them what to do. They want their own governments right here on earth.

What about us? When we learn about God's Kingdom and all the wonderful things that it will do, how does that make us feel toward God?— We love him, don't we?— How, then, can we show God that we do love him and that we want to be ruled by his Kingdom?—

We can show God how we feel by following Jesus' example. And what did Jesus do to show that he loved Jehovah?— "I always do the things pleasing to him," Jesus explained. (John 8: 29) Yes, Jesus came to earth 'to do God's will' and "to finish his work." (Hebrews 10:7; John 4:34) Consider what Jesus did before he began his preaching work.

Jesus went to John the Baptist down at the Jordan River. After they waded into the water, John put Jesus all the way under the water and then lifted him out again. Do you know why John baptized Jesus?—

Jesus asked John to do it. But how do we know that God wanted Jesus to be baptized?— We know that because when Jesus came

Why did Jesus get baptized, and how did God show that he approved?

up out of the water, he heard God's voice from heaven say: "You are my Son, the beloved; I have approved you." God even sent his holy spirit in the form of a dove down upon Jesus. So by being baptized, Jesus showed that he wanted to serve Jehovah all his life, yes, forever.—Mark 1:9-11.

Now you are still growing up. But what are you going to do later?— Will you be like Jesus and get baptized?— You should copy him, for the Bible says he left you "a model for you to follow his steps closely." (1 Peter 2:21) When you do get baptized, you will be showing that you really want to be ruled by God's Kingdom. But it is not enough just to be baptized.

We need to obey all the things that Jesus taught. Jesus said that we should be "no part of the world." Would we be obeying him if we become involved with things of the world? Jesus and his apostles stayed away from such things. (John 17:14) What did they do instead?— They talked to other people about God's Kingdom. That was the big work in their lives. Can we do that too?— Yes, and we will do it if we mean what we say when we pray for God's Kingdom to come.

Please see these other scriptures that tell us what we can do to show that we want God's Kingdom to come: Matthew 6:24-33; 24:14; 1 John 2:15-17; and 5:3.

CHAPTER 46

WATER DESTROYS A WORLD —WILL IT HAPPEN AGAIN?

HAVE you ever heard anyone talk about the end of the world?— Today many do talk about it. Some people think the world will end in a war in which men use nuclear bombs. Do you think God will let people destroy our beautiful earth and our lovely heavens and its shining stars?—

As we have learned, the Bible tells about the end of the world. "The world is passing away," the Bible says. (1 John 2:17) Do you think the end of the world will mean the end of the earth?— No, the Bible says that God made the earth "*to be inhabited*," yes, for people to live on it

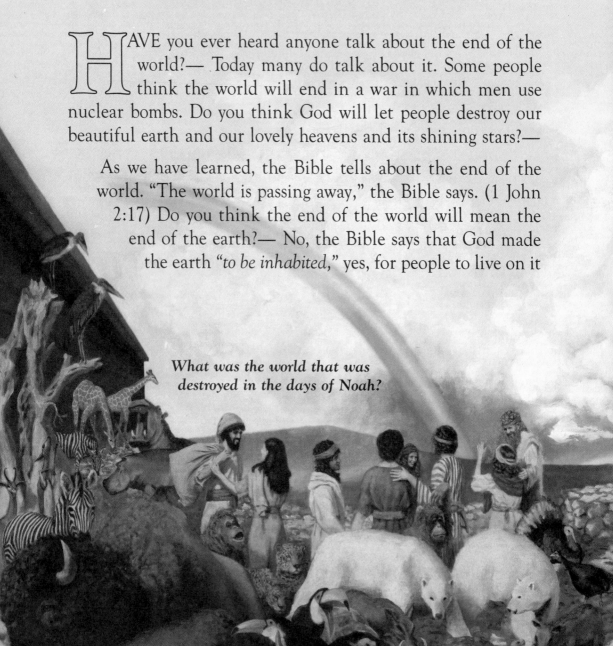

What was the world that was destroyed in the days of Noah?

and to enjoy it. (Isaiah 45:18) Psalm 37:29 says: "The righteous themselves will possess the earth, and they will reside forever upon it." For this reason the Bible also says that the earth will last forever.—Psalm 104:5; Ecclesiastes 1:4.

So if the end of the world does not mean the end of the earth, what does it mean?— We can find out if we look carefully at what happened in the days of Noah. The Bible explains: "*The world of that time suffered destruction* when it was deluged [or, flooded] with water."—2 Peter 3:6.

Did anybody live through the end of the world during that Deluge, or great Flood, in Noah's day?— The Bible says that God "kept Noah, a preacher of righteousness, safe with seven others when he brought a deluge upon a world of ungodly people."—2 Peter 2:5.

So, then, what was the world that ended? Was it the earth, or was it the bad people?— The Bible says that it was the "*world of ungodly people.*" And notice, Noah is called "a preacher." What do you think he was preaching about?— Noah was warning people about the end of "*the world of that time.*"

When Jesus spoke about the great Flood, he told his disciples about what the people had been doing just before the end came. This is what he said to them: "In those days before the flood, [people were] eating and drinking, men marrying and women being given in marriage, until the day that Noah entered into the ark; and *they took no note until the flood came and swept them all away.*" Then Jesus said that people would be acting just like that before this world ends.—Matthew 24:37-39.

Jesus' words show us that we can learn lessons from what the people were doing before the Flood. From reading Chapter 10 of this book, do you remember what those people did?— Some men were bullies and did violent things. But many others, Jesus said, just did not listen when God sent Noah to preach to them.

So the day came when Jehovah told Noah that He was going to destroy the bad people by a flood. The water would cover the whole earth, even the mountains. Jehovah told Noah to build a big ark. It was like a big, long box, or chest, as you can see if you turn back to the picture on page 238.

God told Noah to build the ark big enough to hold him and his family and many of the animals safe inside of it. Noah and his family worked very hard. They cut down large trees, and using the wood they began putting the ark together. This took many, many years because the ark was so large.

Do you remember what else Noah was doing during all the years that he was building the ark?— He was preaching, warning the people about the coming Flood. Did any of them listen? None of them did except Noah's family. The rest were just too busy doing other things. Do you remember what Jesus said they were doing?— They were busy eating and drinking and getting married. They did not think that they were so bad, and they did not take time to listen to Noah. So let's see what happened to them.

After Noah and his family went inside the ark, Jehovah shut the door. People outside still did not believe that the Flood would come. But all of a sudden, water began to fall from the sky! It was not just a regular rain. It was a downpour!

Soon the water was like big rivers, making a lot of noise. It pushed over big trees and rolled big stones as if they were little pebbles. And what about the people outside the ark?— Jesus says: "The flood came and swept them all away." All the people outside the ark died. Why?— As Jesus said, "they took no note." They did not listen!—Matthew 24:39; Genesis 6:5-7.

Now, remember, Jesus said that what happened to those people is a lesson for us today. What lesson can we learn?— Well, people were destroyed not only because they were bad but because many were just too busy to take the time to learn about God and about what he was going to do. We need to be careful that we are not like them, don't we?—

Do you think that God will again destroy the world by a flood?— No, God promised that he wouldn't. He said: "My rainbow I do give in the cloud, and it must serve as a sign." Jehovah said that the rainbow would be a sign that "no more will the waters become a deluge to bring all flesh to ruin."—Genesis 9:11-17.

So we can be sure that God will never again destroy the world by a flood. Yet, as we have seen, the Bible does tell about the end of the world. When God brings the destruction of this world, whom will he keep alive?— Will it be people

Why should we not just be thinking about having fun?

who were so interested in other things that they never wanted to learn about God? Will it be those who were always too busy to study the Bible? What do you think?—

We want to be among those whom God will keep alive, don't we?— Wouldn't it be wonderful if our family could be like Noah's so that God would save all of us?— If we are to survive the end of the world, we need to understand how God will destroy it and bring about his righteous new world. Let's see how he does this.

The Bible gives us the answer at Daniel chapter 2, verse 44. This scripture is speaking about our own day when it says: "In the days of those kings the God of heaven will set up a kingdom [or, government] that will never be brought to ruin. And the kingdom itself will not be passed on to any other people. It will crush and put an end to all these kingdoms, and it itself will stand to times indefinite."

Do you understand that?— The Bible says that God's government is going to destroy all earthly governments. Why?— Because they don't obey the One whom God has made King. And who is that?— Yes, Jesus Christ!

Jehovah God has the right to decide what kind of government should rule, and he has chosen his Son, Jesus, to be King. Soon God's Ruler, Jesus Christ, will take the lead in destroying all the governments of this world. The Bible, at Revelation chapter 19, verses 11 to 16, describes him as he does so, even as this picture shows. In the Bible, God's war to destroy all the governments of the world is called Har–Magedon, or Armageddon.

Now, God says that his Kingdom will destroy the governments of men. But does he tell us to do that?— No, in the Bible, Armageddon is called "the war of the great day of God the Almighty." (Revelation 16:14, 16) Yes, Armageddon is God's war, and he uses Jesus Christ to lead the heavenly armies in the fight. Is the war of Armageddon near? Let's see how we can find out.

Let's read together about when God gets rid of all the wicked and saves those who serve him, at Proverbs 2:21, 22; Isaiah 26:20, 21; Jeremiah 25:31-33; and Matthew 24:21, 22.

Jesus Christ, God's chosen King, will destroy this world at Armageddon

CHAPTER 47

HOW WE CAN TELL ARMAGEDDON IS NEAR

YOU know what a sign is, don't you?— In Chapter 46 we read about the sign God gave that he would never again destroy the world by a flood. Also, the apostles asked for a sign so that they could know when Jesus had returned and when the end of the world, or system of things, was near. —Matthew 24:3.

Since Jesus would be invisible in heaven, a sign that people could see was needed to show that he had begun ruling. So Jesus told about things his disciples should watch for here on earth. When these things happened, it would mean that he had returned and had begun ruling in heaven as King.

To teach his disciples the importance of keeping on the watch, Jesus told them: "Note the fig tree and all the other trees: When

What lesson was Jesus teaching when he talked about the fig tree?

244

they are already in the bud, *by observing it* you know for yourselves that now the summer is near." You know how to tell when summer is near. And you can tell when Armageddon is near when you see the things happening that Jesus spoke about.—Luke 21:29, 30.

On this page and the following one, we are going to look at pictures of things that Jesus said would be part of the sign that the Kingdom of God is near. When all these things occur,

God's Kingdom with Christ as Ruler will crush all other governments, as we read in Chapter 46.

So look carefully at the pictures on the two pages before this one, and we will talk about them. At Matthew 24:6-14 and Luke 21:9-11, you can read about what you see in these pictures. Also, notice the small number on each picture. The same number is found at the beginning of the paragraph that describes that picture. Now let's see if the many parts of the sign that Jesus gave are being fulfilled today.

(1) Jesus said: *"You are going to hear of wars and reports of wars; . . . nation will rise against nation and kingdom against kingdom."* Have you heard reports about wars?— The first world war was fought from 1914 to 1918, and then there was World War II, from 1939 to 1945. Never before had there been world wars! Now there are wars all over the world. It seems that every day on TV, on the radio, and in the newspaper, we hear or read about wars.

(2) Jesus also said: *"There will be food shortages . . . in one place after another."* As you may know, not everyone has enough food to eat. Every day thousands of people die because they do not have enough food.

(3) Jesus added: *'In one place after another there will be pestilences.'* Do you know what a pestilence is?— It is a sickness, or disease, that kills many people. One great pestilence called the Spanish flu killed about 20 million people within just a year or so. In our day more people than that will probably die from AIDS. And there are cancer, heart disease, and other sicknesses that kill many thousands of people every year.

(4) Jesus gave another part of the sign, saying: *"There will be . . . earthquakes in one place after another."* Do you know what an earthquake is?— Earthquakes make the ground shake under your feet. Houses fall down, and people often get killed. Since the year 1914, there have been many earthquakes every year. Have you heard about earthquakes?—

(5) Jesus said that another part of the sign would be 'more and more badness.' That is why there is so much stealing and violence. People everywhere are afraid that someone might try to break into their homes. Never before has there been as much crime and violence in all parts of the world as there is now.

(6) Jesus gave a very important part of the sign when he said: *"This good news of the kingdom will be preached in all the inhabited earth for a witness to all the nations; and then the end will come."* (Matthew 24:14) If you believe "this good news," then you should talk about it to others. In that way you can share in fulfilling this part of the sign.

Some people may say that the things Jesus foretold have always happened. But never before have such things *all* happened in so many parts of the world and at the same time. So do you understand what the sign means?— It means that when we see all these things happening, this wicked world will soon be replaced by God's new world.

When Jesus gave this sign, he also spoke of a special season of the year. He said: "Keep praying that your flight may not occur in wintertime." (Matthew 24:20) What do you think he meant by that?—

Well, if a person has to escape some disaster during the winter, when the weather makes it very hard or even dangerous to travel, what could happen?— If he escaped at all, it would be with great difficulty. Wouldn't it be sad for someone to die in a winter storm just because he was too busy doing other things to start his journey earlier?—

Do you see the point Jesus was making by talking about not waiting until wintertime to flee?— He was telling us that since we know that Armageddon is near, we do not want to delay in taking action to prove we love God by serving him. If we delay, it may be too late for us. So we would be just like those at the time of the great Flood who heard Noah but did not get inside the ark.

Next, let's talk about what it will be like when the great war of Armageddon is over. We will learn what God has in store for all of us who love and serve him now.

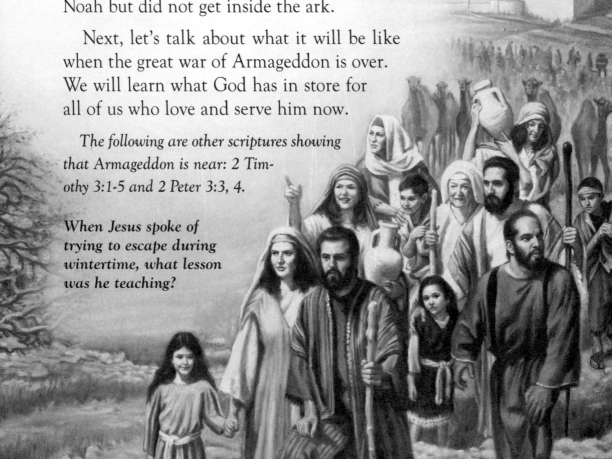

The following are other scriptures showing that Armageddon is near: 2 Timothy 3:1-5 and 2 Peter 3:3, 4.

When Jesus spoke of trying to escape during wintertime, what lesson was he teaching?

CHAPTER 48

GOD'S PEACEFUL NEW WORLD —YOU CAN LIVE THERE

GOD put Adam and Eve in the garden of Eden. Even though they became disobedient and died, God has made it possible for their children, including us today, to live forever in Paradise. The Bible promises: "The righteous themselves will possess the earth, and they will [live] forever upon it."—Psalm 37:29.

The Bible tells about a "new heavens" and "a new earth." (Isaiah 65:17; 2 Peter 3:13) The present "heavens" are made up of today's human governments, but Jesus Christ and those who rule with him in heaven will make up the "new heavens." How wonderful it will be when this new heavens, which is God's righteous government of peace, rules the entire earth!

What, then, is the "new earth"?— The new earth will be good people who love Jehovah. You see, when the Bible speaks of "the earth," it sometimes means the people who live on the earth, not the land itself. (Genesis 11:1; Psalm 66:4; 96:1) So the people who make up the new earth will live right here on this earth.

The present world of wicked people will then be gone. Remember, the Flood of Noah's day wiped out a wicked world of people. And, as we have learned, this present wicked world will be destroyed at Armageddon. Let's see now what it will be like to live in God's new world after Armageddon.

As you read Isaiah 11:6-9 and Isaiah 65:25, you learn about animals living in peace. Look at these pictures. See the lamb, the little goat, the leopard, the calf, the big lion, and the children with them. Can you name the other animals here that the Bible talks about?— Look at that boy playing with the cobra! No one living in the new world needs to be afraid. (Hosea 2:18) What do you think about that?—

Now, see the peace among people of all kinds.
They all love one another, as Jesus said his
followers would. (John 13:34, 35) Weapons of
war are being made into tools to take care
of the earth. The Bible tells about the
wonderful peace and security that people
will enjoy in God's new world. We can
read about this in such scriptures
as Psalm 72:7; Isaiah 2:4;
32:16-18; and Ezekiel 34:25.

See the people on this page. They are caring for the earth, making it a beautiful place. Look at the nice house they are building and all the good fruits and vegetables shown here. People are at peace with the earth, so it has become a paradise like the garden of Eden. We can read about these wonderful things at Psalm 67:6; 72:16; Isaiah 25:6; 65:21-24; and Ezekiel 36:35.

As you see here, everybody is healthy and happy. People can jump high like a deer. Nobody is lame, blind, or sick. And see those people who have been raised from the dead! The Bible tells about these things at Isaiah 25:8; 33:24; 35:5, 6; Acts 24:15; and Revelation 21:3, 4.

Do you want to live forever in Paradise in God's peaceful new world?— No doctor can make us live forever. There is no pill that will keep us from dying. The only way we can live forever is by drawing close to God. And the Great Teacher tells us how to do that.

Let's get our Bibles and open them to John chapter 17, verse 3. Here we find these words of the Great Teacher: "This means everlasting life, their taking in knowledge of you, the only true God, and of the one whom you sent forth, Jesus Christ."

So, what did Jesus say we need to do to live forever?— First, we must take in knowledge of our heavenly Father, Jehovah, and also of his Son, who gave his life for us. This means that we need to study the Bible. This book, *Learn From the Great Teacher*, is helping us to do that.

But how will learning about Jehovah help us to live forever?— Well, just as we need food every day, we need to learn about Jehovah every day. The Bible says: 'Man must live, not on bread alone, but on all the words that come from Jehovah's mouth.'—Matthew 4:4.

We also need to take in knowledge of Jesus Christ because God sent his Son to take away our sin. The Bible says: "There is no salvation in anyone else." And the Bible also says: "He that exercises faith in the Son has everlasting life." (Acts 4:12; John 3:36) Now, what does it mean to 'exercise faith' in Jesus?— It means that we really believe in Jesus and know that we cannot live forever without him. Do we believe that?— If we do, we will continue to learn from the Great Teacher every day, and we will do what he says.

One fine way to learn from the Great Teacher is to read this book over and over and to look at and think about all the pictures. See if you can answer the questions found with these pictures. Also, read the book with your mother or father. If your parents are not with you, read it with other grown-ups and with other children. Wouldn't it be wonderful if you could help others to learn from the Great Teacher what they need to do to live forever in God's new world?—

The Bible tells us: "The world is passing away." But then the Bible explains how we can live forever in God's new world. It says: "He that does the will of God remains forever." (1 John 2:17) So how can we live forever in God's new world?— Yes, by taking in knowledge of Jehovah and his dear Son, Jesus. But we also have to do, or practice, what we learn. May your study of this book help you to do these things.

Would you welcome more information?
Write Jehovah's Witnesses at the appropriate address below.

ALASKA 99507: 2552 East 48th Ave., Anchorage. **AUSTRALIA:** Box 280, Ingleburn, NSW 1890. **BAHAMAS:** Box N-1247, Nassau, N.P. **BARBADOS, W.I.:** Crusher Site Road, Prospect, St. James. **BRITAIN:** The Ridgeway, London NW7 1RN. **CANADA:** Box 4100, Halton Hills (Georgetown), Ontario L7G 4Y4. **FIJI:** Box 23, Suva. **GERMANY:** Niederselters, Am Steinfels, D-65618 Selters. **GHANA:** P. O. Box GP 760, Accra. **GUYANA:** 50 Brickdam, Georgetown 16. **HAWAII 96819:** 2055 Kam IV Rd., Honolulu. **HONG KONG:** 4 Kent Road, Kowloon Tong. **INDIA:** Post Box No. 6440, Yelahanka, Bangalore 560 064, KAR. **IRELAND:** Newcastle, Greystones, Co. Wicklow. **JAMAICA:** P. O. Box 103, Old Harbour, St. Catherine. **JAPAN:** 1271 Nakashinden, Ebina City, Kanagawa Pref., 243-0496. **KENYA:** P. O. Box 47788, GPO Nairobi 00100. **LIBERIA:** P. O. Box 10-0380, 1000 Monrovia 10. **MALAYSIA:** Peti Surat No. 580, 75760 Melaka. **NEW ZEALAND:** P O Box 75-142, Manurewa. **NIGERIA:** P.M.B. 1090, Benin City 300001, Edo State. **PANAMA:** Apartado 6-2671, Zona 6A, El Dorado. **PAPUA NEW GUINEA:** P. O. Box 636, Boroko, NCD 111. **PHILIPPINES, REPUBLIC OF:** P. O. Box 2044, 1060 Manila. **SOUTH AFRICA:** Private Bag X2067, Krugersdorp, 1740. **SWITZERLAND:** P.O. Box 225, CH-3602 Thun. **TRINIDAD AND TOBAGO, REP. OF:** Lower Rapsey Street & Laxmi Lane, Curepe. **UNITED STATES OF AMERICA:** 25 Columbia Heights, Brooklyn, NY 11201-2483. **ZAMBIA:** Box 33459, Lusaka 10101. **ZIMBABWE:** Private Bag WG-5001, Westgate.